MW00776728

Optavia Diet for Women Over 50

The Complete Guide to Optavia Diet Lifestyle | Regain your Metabolism, Uncover Boundless Energy, and Quickly Shed Weight

Text Copyright © [Betty Barnard]

All rights reserved. No part of this guide may be reproduced in any form without permission in writing from the publisher except in the case of brief quotations embodied in critical articles or reviews.

Legal & Disclaimer

The information contained in this book and its contents is not designed to replace or take the place of any form of medical or professional advice; and is not meant to replace the need for independent medical, financial, legal or other professional advice or services, as may be required. The content and information in this book has been provided for educational and entertainment purposes only.

The content and information contained in this book has been compiled from sources deemed reliable, and it is accurate to the best of the Author's knowledge, information and belief. However, the Author cannot guarantee its accuracy and validity and cannot be held liable for any errors and/or omissions. Further, changes are periodically made to this book as and when needed. Where appropriate and/or necessary, you must consult a professional (including but not limited to your doctor, attorney, financial advisor or such other professional advisor) before using any of the suggested remedies, techniques, or information in this book.

Upon using the contents and information contained in this book, you agree to hold harmless the Author from and against any damages, costs, and expenses, including any legal fees potentially resulting from the application of any of the information provided by this book. This disclaimer applies to any loss, damages or injury caused by the use and application, whether directly or indirectly, of any advice or information presented, whether for breach of contract, tort, negligence, personal injury, criminal intent, or under any other cause of action.

You agree to accept all risks of using the information presented inside this book.

You agree that by continuing to read this book, where appropriate and/or necessary, you shall consult a professional (including but not limited to your doctor, attorney, or financial advisor or such other advisor as needed) before using any of the suggested remedies, techniques, or information in this book.

Table of Contents

Introduction

The Optavia Diet isn't expected for a particular crowd, however it will in general intrigue to individuals who need to quit "overthinking" an eating plan.

Optavia will in general be a most loved among individuals with a bustling way of life, yet the arrangement's decreased calorie approach is expected for anybody hoping to lose weight.

Consumers have for quite some time been attracted to the comfort of meal substitution and abstain from food that does not help in weight reduction. One famous meal substitution plan is the Optavia Diet. It aims to assist individuals with getting more fit by consuming modest quantities of calories for the duration of the day. To assist you with choosing if the program could assist you with accomplishing your weight reduction objectives, here's a gander at how the Optavia Diet functions, just as the plan pro and con.

How It Works

Like other meal substitution consumes less calories, the Optavia Diet furnishes clients with its own variety of marked items that replace a few meals for the duration of the day. You will do a mix of what OPTAVIA calls "fuelings" and meals you set yourself up. Depending on your requirements, needs, way of life and your spending you can choose a couple of various program choices. Notwithstanding which program you pick, it will help you through the procedure and assist you with building long term, reasonable habits. Numerous weight control plans can assist you with getting results, yet OPTAVIA additionally needs you to support your outcomes.

Optavia offers diet plans for objectives of weight loss and weight support.

Chapter 1: Optavia Diet compliance food

Dietary control, including protein, phosphorus, and sodium limitation, when combined with the veggie lover nature of the renal eating regimen and ketoacid supplementation can conceivably apply a cardiovascular defensive impact in perpetual renal disappointment patients by following up on both conventional and nontraditional cardiovascular hazard factors.

Circulatory strain control might be supported by the decrease of sodium consumption and by the vegan idea of the eating routine, which is significant likewise for bringing down serum cholesterol and improving plasma lipid profile. The low protein and phosphorus admission have a significant job for decreasing proteinuria and forestalling and switching hyperphosphatemia and auxiliary hyperparathyroidism, which are real reasons for the vascular calcifications, cardiovascular harm, and mortality danger of uremic patients.

The decrease of nitrogenous waste items and bringing down of serum PTH levels may likewise help enhance insulin affectability and metabolic control in diabetic patients, just as increment the responsiveness to erythropoietin treatment, accordingly permitting more noteworthy control of iron deficiency. Protein-limited eating regimens may have likewise calming and against oxidant properties.

Accordingly, setting aside the still begging to be proven wrong consequences for the movement of renal ailment and the more conceded impacts on uremic signs and side effects, it is conceivable that an appropriate healthful treatment right off the bat over the span of renal sickness might be helpful additionally to diminish the cardiovascular hazard in the renal patient. Be that as it may, definitive information can't yet be drawn on the grounds that quality investigations are deficient in this field; future examinations ought to be intended to evaluate the impact of renal eating regimens on hard results, as cardiovascular occasions or mortality.

Basic principles

The general principles of diet treatment for chronic kidney patients are as follows:

- Limit protein intake to 0.8 gm/kg per kilogram per day for non-dialysis patients. Patients on dialysis need a greater amount of protein to compensate for the possible loss of proteins during the procedure. (1.0 to 1.2 gm/kg daily according to body weight)

- Taking enough carbohydrates to provide energy.

- Taking normal amounts of oil. Reduction of butter, pure fat, and oil intake.
- Restriction of fluid and water intake in case of swelling (edema).
- Dietary intake of sodium, potassium, and phosphorus limitation.
- Taking adequate amounts of vitamins and trace elements. A high-fiber diet is recommended.

High-Calorie Intake

The details of the selection and modification of the diet for chronic kidney patients are as follows:

High-Calorie Intake

In addition to daily activities, the body needs calories to maintain heat, growth, and adequate body weight. Calories are taken with carbohydrates and fats. The daily normal calorie intake of patients suffering from chronic kidney disease according to body weight is 35-40 kcal/kg. If caloric intake is insufficient, the body uses proteins to provide calories. Such distribution of the protein may cause deleterious effects, such as improper nutrition and increased production of waste materials. Therefore, it is very important to provide enough calories to CKD patients. It is important to calculate the patient's daily calorie requirement based on the ideal body weight, not the current weight.

Carbohydrates

Carbohydrates are the primary source of calories required for the body. Carbohydrates, wheat, cereals, rice, potatoes, fruits and vegetables, sugar, honey, cookies, pastry, confectionery, and beverages. Diabetes and obesity patients should limit the number of carbohydrates. It is best to make use of complex carbohydrates that can be obtained from whole grains such as whole wheat or raw rice that can provide fiber. They should constitute a large part of the number of carbohydrates in the diet. The proportion of all other sugar-containing substances should not exceed 20% of the total carbohydrate intake, particularly in diabetic patients. As long as chocolate, hazelnut, or banana desserts are consumed in a limited amount, non-diabetic patients may be replaced with calories, fruit, pies, pastry, cookies, and protein.

Oils

Chronic kidney patients should limit the intake of saturated fat and cholesterol that may cause heart disease. In the case of unsaturated fat, it is necessary to pay attention to the proportion of monounsaturated fat and polyunsaturated fat. Excessive uptake of omega-6 polyunsaturated fatty acids (CFAs) and a relatively high omega-6 / omega-3 ratio are detrimental, while the low omega-6 / omega-3 ratio has beneficial effects. The use of vegetable oils instead of uniform oils will achieve this goal. Trans fat-containing substances such as potato chips, sweet buns, instant cookies, and pastries are extremely dangerous and should be avoided.

Restriction of Protein Intake

Protein is essential for the restoration and maintenance of body tissues. It also helps to heal wounds and fight infection. In patients with chronic renal failure who do not undergo dialysis, protein limitation is recommended to reduce the rate of decrease in renal function and postpone the need for dialysis and renal transplantation. (<0.8 gm/kg daily according to body weight). However, excessive protein restriction should also be avoided due to the risk of malnutrition.

Anorexia is a common condition in patients with chronic kidney disease. Strict protein restriction, poor diet, weight loss, fatigue, and loss of body resistance as well as loss of appetite; this increases the risk of death. High protein proteins such as animal protein (meat, poultry, and fish), eggs, and tofu are preferred. Chronic kidney patients should avoid high protein diets (e.g. the Atkins diet). Similarly, protein supplements or medications such as creatinine used for muscle development should be avoided unless recommended by a physician or dietician. However, as the patient begins dialysis, daily protein intake should be increased by 1.0 to 1.2 gm/kg body weight to recover the proteins lost during the procedure.

Fluid intake

Why should chronic kidney patients take precautions about fluid intake?

The kidneys maintain the correct amount of water in the body by removing excess liquid as urea. In patients with chronic kidney disease, the urea volume usually decreases as the kidney functions deteriorate. Reduction of urea excretion from the body causes fluid retention in the body, resulting in facial swelling, swelling of legs and hands, and high blood pressure. Accumulation of fluid causes shortness of breath and difficulty breathing. This can be life-threatening if not checked.

What precautions should chronic kidney patients take to control fluid intake?

To prevent overloading or loss of fluid, the amount of fluid taken on the advice of a physician should be recorded and monitored. The amount of water to be taken for each chronic kidney patient may vary, and this rate is calculated according to the urea excretion and fluid status of each patient.

What is the recommended amount of fluid for patients with chronic kidney disease?

Unlimited edema and water intake can be done in patients who do not have edema and who can throw enough urea from the body. The recommended amount of fluid depends on the patient's clinical condition and renal function.

Patients with edema who cannot appoint enough urea from the body should limit fluid intake. To reduce swelling, fluid intake within 24 hours should be less than the amount of urine produced by the daily body.

In patients with edema, the amount of fluid that should be taken daily should be 500 ml more than the previous day's urine volume to prevent fluid overload or fluid loss. This additional 500 ml of liquid will approximately compensate for the fluids lost by perspiration and exhalation.

Why should chronic kidney patients keep a record of their daily weight?

Patients should record of their weight daily to detect fluid increase or loss or to monitor fluid volume in their bodies. Body weight will remain constant if the instructions for fluid intake are strictly followed. Sudden weight gain indicates excessive fluid overload due to increased fluid intake in the body. Weight gain is a warning that the patient should make more rigorous fluid restriction. Weight loss is usually caused by fluid restriction and the use of diuretics.

Useful Tips for Restricting Fluid Intake

Reduce salty, spicy, or fried foods in your diet because these foods can increase your thirst and cause more fluid consumption.

Only for water when you are thirsty. Do not drink as a habit or because of everyone drinks.

When thirsty, consume only a small amount of water or try ice — sure taking a little ice cube. Ice stays in the mouth longer than water so that it will give a more satisfying result than the same amount of water. Remember to calculate the amount of liquid consumed. To calculate simply, freeze the amount of water allocated for drinking in the ice block.

To prevent dry mouth, gargle with water, but do not swallow the water. Dry mouth can also be reduced by chewing gum, sucking hard candies, lemon slices or mint candies and using a small amount of water to moisturize your mouth.

Always use small cups or glasses to limit fluid intake. Instead of consuming extra water for medication use, take your medicines while drinking water after meals.

The patient should engage himself in a job. Patients who are not engaged in a job often desire to drink water.

High blood sugar in diabetic patients can increase the level of thirst. To reduce thirst, it is essential to keep blood sugar under tight control.

Since the person's thirst increases in hot weather, measures to be in cooler environments may be preferred and recommended.

Chapter 2: Steps To Follow The Optavia Diet

Notwithstanding the course of action you pick, you start by having a phone conversation with a coach to help make sense of which Optavia plan to follow, set weight decrease goals, and familiarize yourself with the program.

On this plan, you eat 5 Optavia Fuelings and 1 Lean and Green supper step by step. You're proposed to eat 1 dining experience every 2–3 hours and merge 30 minutes of moderate exercise most days of the week.

By and large, the Fuelings and supper offer near 100 grams of carbs consistently.

You demand these dinners from your coach's individual site, as Optavia tutors get paid on commission.

This game plan also joins 1 optional snack for every day, which must be embraced by your guide. Plan-confirmed bites fuse 3 celery sticks, 1/2 cup (60 grams) of without sugar gelatin, or 1/2 ounce (14 grams) of nuts.

The program also fuses an eating out guide that reveals how to orchestrate a Lean and Green banquet at your favored restaurant. Recall that alcohol is unequivocally incapacitated on the 5&1 Plan.

Upkeep stage

At the point when you show up at your optimal weight, you enter a 6-week change stage, which incorporates continuously extending calories to near 1,550 calories for consistently and blending it up of sustenances, including whole grains, regular items, and low fat dairy.

Following a month and a half, you're planned to move onto the Optimal Health 3&3 Plan, which consolidate 3 Lean and Green suppers and 3 Fuelings step by step, notwithstanding continued Optavia preparing.

The people who experience proceeded with achievement on the program have the choice to get readied as an Optavia coach.

Blueprint to follow

The Optavia 5&1 weight decrease plan is low in calories and carbs and fuses five prepackaged Fuelings and one low carb Lean and Green supper consistently. At the point when you achieve your goal weight, you progress into a less restrictive help plan.

Would it have the option to help you with getting more fit?

The Optavia diet is expected to help people with shedding pounds and fat by diminishing calories and carbs through part controlled dinners and nibbles.

The 5&1 game plan limits calories to 800–1,000 calories for every day isolated between 6 parceled controlled suppers.

While the assessment is mixed, a couple of examinations have shown more essential weight decrease with full or partial blowout overriding plans differentiated and standard calorie-restricted diets.

Studies moreover reveal that reducing as a rule calorie confirmation is ground-breaking for weight and fat adversity — as are low carb diets, in any occasion briefly.

A 16-week move in 198 people with excess weight or chunkiness found that those on Optavia's 5&1 Plan had basically lower weight, fat levels, and midsection circuit, differentiated and the benchmark gathering.

All things considered, with 28.1% of individuals losing over 10%. This may suggest additional preferences, as investigation accomplices' 5–10% weight decrease with a lessened risk of coronary ailment. A comparable report found that individuals on the 5&1 diet who completed in any occasion 75% of the educating gatherings lost more than twice as much weight as the people who looked into less gatherings.

Nonetheless, you ought to recall that this examination was sponsored by Medifast.

The same, a couple of various assessments show a gigantic improvement in short-and long stretch weight decrease and diet adherence in programs that join advancing educating

At present, no examinations have broke down the drawn out eventual outcomes of the Optavia diet. Taking everything into account, an assessment on an equivalent Medifast plan saw that solitary 25% of individuals kept up the diet for up to 1 year.

Another test gave some weight recuperate during the weight uphold stage following the 5&1 Medifast diet.

Chapter 3: Pros and Cons of Optavia Diet

Pros

•Packaged items offer comfort

•Achieves fast weight reduction

•Takes away guesswork on exactly mystery what to eat

•Offers social help

Cons

•High month to month cost

•Includes a great deal of prepared food

•Weight lose may not be sustainable

•Calorie limitation may leave you ravenous or exhausted

•Mealtimes can get exhausting or feel disconnecting

Pros

Optavia's program may be a solid match for you in the event that you need an eating routine arrangement that is clear and simple to follow, that will assist you with getting more fit rapidly, and offers worked in social help.

Packaged Products comes with real Convenience

Optavia's shakes, soups, and all other food substitution items are conveyed straightforwardly to your door—a degree of comfort that numerous different weight control plans don't offer.

Despite the fact that you should look for your own elements for "lean and green" foods, the home conveyance alternative for Optavia's "fuelings" spares time and vitality.

When the items show up, they're anything but difficult to plan and make astounding snatch and-go dinners.

Accomplishes Rapid Weight Loss

The average calorie consumption for a normal healthy person is around 1600 to 3000 calories for each day to keep up their weight. Limiting that number to as low as 800 basically ensures weight reduction for the vast majority.

Optavia's 5 and 1 arrangement is intended for speedy weight reduction, making it a strong choice for somebody with a clinical motivation to shed pounds quick.

Eliminates every form of Guesswork

A few people find that the hardest piece of counting calories is the psychological exertion required to make sense of what to eat every day—or even at every dinner.

Provides Social Support

Social help is an indispensable part of accomplishment with any weight reduction plan. Optavia's training project and gathering calls give worked in consolation and support for clients.

Cons

There are likewise some expected drawbacks to Optavia's arrangement, particularly on the off chance that you are stressed over cost, adaptability, and assortment.

High Monthly Cost

Optavia's expense can be an obstruction for imminent clients. The 5 and 1 arrangement runs in cost from $350 to $425 for 119 servings (around three weeks of supper substitutions).

As you're thinking about the program's expense, remember to factor in the food you'll have to buy to set up your "lean and green" dinners.

Incorporates Processed Food

In spite of the fact that Optavia's "fuelings" are built with exchangeable supplements, they're still obviously prepared nourishments, which might be a mood killer for certain clients.

Nourishment research has demonstrated eating a ton of handled food can effectsly affect one's wellbeing, so this part of the eating routine arrangement may represent a burden.

Weight reduction May Not Be Sustainable

One test recognizable to anybody on a careful nutritional plan is deciding how to keep up weight reduction once they've finished the program.

The equivalent goes for Optavia's program. At the point when clients return to eating ordinary dinners rather than the arrangement's feast substitutions, they may find that the weight they lost is immediately recaptured.

Summary of the Advantages and disadvantages of Weight Watchers

Advantages

•Balanced and adaptable

•Tons of help and assets

•Reduces diabetes hazard

•Promotes work out

•Teaches long lasting abilities

•No nourishments are illegal

•Slow and consistent weight reduction

Disadvantages

•Can be expensive

•Counting points can be monotonous

•Weekly weigh-ins are essential

•Limited proof for cardiovascular advantages

•Too much opportunity for certain individuals

•May lead to unfortunate abstaining from excessive food intake

Calorie Restriction Impact

Regardless of the way that Optavia's eating routine plan stresses eating once in a while for the span of the day, all of its "fuelings" just gives 110 calories. "Lean and green" nourishments are furthermore low in calories.

Exactly when you're eating less calories with everything taken into account, you may find the game plan leaves you insatiable and unsatisfied. You may in like manner feel even more adequately depleted and even bad tempered.

Optavia's training portion is like Weight Watchers and Jenny Craig, the two of which ask individuals to choose in for meetups to get social assistance.

The astoundingly taken care of nature of most foods you'll eat on the Optavia diet can be a disadvantage appeared differently in relation to the assortment of new, whole foods you can eat on progressively autonomously coordinated plans, for instance, Atkins.

Chapter 4: Benefits Of Optavia Diet

The Optavia diet has additional focal points that may uphold weight decrease and when all is said in done prosperity.

Steps to follow

As the diet relies generally upon prepackaged Fuelings, you're only subject for setting one up supper for consistently on the 5&1 Plan.

Moreover, every plan goes with dinner logs and test supper expects to make it less complex to follow.

While you're asked to cook 1–3 Lean and Green suppers consistently, dependent upon the course of action, they're anything but difficult to make — as the program joins express plans and a once-over of food choices.

Also, the people who aren't enthusiastic about getting ready can buy packaged dinners called Flavors of Home to displace Lean and Green suppers.

May improve blood circulatory

Optavia ventures may help improve circulatory strain through weight decrease and confined sodium utilization.

While the Optavia diet hasn't been investigated expressly, a 40-week move in 90 people with excess weight or heaviness on a similar Medifast program revealed a tremendous abatement in circulatory strain.

Additionally, all Optavia feast plans are expected to give under 2,300 mg of sodium for consistently — regardless of the way that it's reliant upon you to pick low sodium decisions for Lean and Green dinners.

Different prosperity affiliations, including the Institute of Medicine, American Heart Association, and United States Department of Agriculture (USDA), recommend using under 2,300 mg of sodium for every day.

That is because higher sodium affirmation is associated with an extended threat of hypertension and coronary disease in salt-delicate individuals.

Offers advancing help

Optavia's prosperity guides are available all through the weight decrease and upkeep programs.

As noted more than, one examination found an essential association between the amount of training gatherings on the Optavia 5&1 Plan and improved weight decrease.

In addition, research suggests that having a lifestyle coach or promoter may help long stretch weight uphold.

Chapter 5: Can it help you lose weight?

The benefit of Optavia diet is that, it targets fat deposit in the most difficult parts of the body, most especially the abdominal region, thighs and the upper chest areas. Starving yourself may not help cut fat in the most difficult regions, even when you lose fat in such areas, they may return quickly, but this is not the case with Optavia diets. Losing weight around your mid-section and around vital organs is necessary in order to avoid serious fat-related diseases.

Optavia diets increases the amount of HDL cholesterols while reducing LDL cholesterol levels. Choosing the right type of unsaturated fats in your Optavia diet will help increase good cholesterols (HDL cholesterols), and these are healthy for the heart and general wellbeing. Optavia diets also help regulate blood sugar levels while reducing the risks of insulin intolerance. When carbs are broken down, they release sugar into the blood quickly and this increases blood sugar rapidly, a condition that triggers more supply of Insulin hormones, but when Optavia diets replace high carb diets, less sugar are released slowly into the body, a situation that can stabilize the secretion of Insulin hormones.

Optavia diet was coined out of the word "Ketosis", a process whereby the body breaks down more fat into fatty acids and ketones. The breakdown of more fats and ketones will provide sufficient energy sources for the body. Free fatty acids and ketones are simultaneously released in into the body during Optavia breakdown, these are then made available for the body to burn as fuel.

Normally, the body relies on Glucose as the main source of energy, however, glucose is released when the body breaks down carbs, but the bad side of relying on glucose for energy is that, it can be readily stored as fat in fat cells, organs and tissues, when the energy is not used up. On the other hand, starving the body of glucose will force it to use stored fat in your organs as a source of fuel, even before they are stored for too long inside the body. With the burning of more ketones and fatty acids, there will be less glucose in the body to burn and the body will rapidly adjust to Optavia phase of deriving energy.

You need to have it in mind that the body can only burn the source of energy present, therefore, constantly consuming Optavia diet will make fats and proteins readily available as source of energy, as opposed to carbs. Optavia diets are effective in two ways, first, they create a net balance of energy in the body, and secondly, they rapidly fill you up (increase satiety), thus, you consume much less than necessary.

With Optavia diet, you have to avoid or limit your consumption of carbs to less than 5% of your daily dietary intake. Secondly, you need to avoid unhealthy carbs such as tubers, starches, sugar and other processes foods.

How does Optavia diet helps you lose weight?

What your body is designed to eat will definitely affect whether you lose weight or not. The earliest humans often rely on what they get during hunting to survive, these include; edible foods, fish and meat, with little or no starch or carb, and that is one of the reasons why they stay slimmer and healthier. With the discovery of processed foods in the modern world (including pasta, white bread and sugary drinks), our bodies have been re-constructed to adjust to such unhealthy lifestyles.

One problem with most starch and sugar is that they can be converted into simple sugars that can be absorbed readily in the blood stream, and the effect of this is that there is a rapid increase in blood sugar level, a condition that triggers a sharp increase in the secretion of Insulin hormones, and this increases the risk of developing diseases such as diabetes type II through rapid weight gain and obesity.

One problem with carbs and sugars is that they increase your cravings, while Optavia diet helps you feel fuller quickly and reduce them. You can be at a dinner with a few friends and they want to share an appetizer and you think one won't hurt, or they want to drink so you figure one drink won't have too many carbs or something along those lines. A quick tip though; a lot of drinks do have carbs and on an Optavia diet, it is really not recommended because you'll bust straight through your numbers. Some people even give in to the peer pressure because their friends get upset that someone is not eating like the rest of them. The early men consume more of Optavia diets, and that is why they consume much less but get more energy for hunting expenditures. Optavia diets helps lower your body's reliance on insulin hormones, and then makes it easier for the body to use up its fat reservoir as a source of energy.

You don't have to starve yourself to enjoy the benefits of Optavia diet, likewise, there is no need to start counting those calories.

Starting A Optavia Diet.

Starting out on any new diet can be hard, but a Optavia diet can be one of the hardest to start. This is because it is a sudden change to a completely different way of eating. Carbs are everywhere and we are programmed to eat as many as we can, so most of us have not had a carb-free day in our entire lives. For this reason, regardless of whether we are starting by reducing our carbs, or going cold turkey, the first few days need to be as easy as possible.

Next, you will want to start on a morning, when you are not going to work. Stress makes us crave carbs more, and eating carbs is what starts the hunger cycle in the first place. You can be at a dinner with a few friends and they want to share an appetizer and you think one won't hurt, or they want to drink so you figure one drink won't have too many carbs or something along those lines. A quick tip though; a lot of drinks do have carbs and on an Optavia diet, it is really not recommended because you'll bust straight through your numbers. Some people even give in to the peer pressure because their friends get upset that someone is not eating like the rest of them. So, if we start with an empty stomach, running on ketones from the previous night, and we are going to have a relaxed day or two, we will be able to stick it out through the first few days. This massively improves our chances of success, as the first days are the hardest.

When you start a Optavia diet, you will find many side effects. Most of them are harmless and just part of your body recovering from a lifetime on a high carb diet. Carb cravings are the most common symptom. We have already discussed why these happen, so it is important to remain calm and try and push through. In the next chapter we will offer some solutions for these hunger pangs but remember that they are at their worst for only a few days, and after that they will be gone.

Indigestion can occur when you first start an Optavia diet. This is due to a common mistake people make, assuming that this diet is low in all plants. That is not true. On this diet you will eat large amounts of high fiber, low carb plant foods, fatty fruits like avocado, and nuts and seeds. If you do not eat enough fiber you will find that your meals cause reflux, indigestion, and gut cramping. If you are eating plenty of plants but still suffering reflux, indigestion, and gut cramping, consider eliminating dairy from your diet. Sometimes following an Optavia diet can make an underlying cow milk protein allergy come to the surface. You always would have had this allergy, but it would have been masked by other aspects of your diet.

Finally, if you suffer stomach cramps, diarrhea, or oily, black stools, then you are eating too much fat. How is it possible to eat too much fat on a low carb, high fat diet? The same way it is possible to pour too much water into a glass. When we are following a Optavia diet we are using fat as fuel. But we can only absorb so much fat in one go and burn so much fat. You can be at a dinner with a few friends and they want to share an appetizer and you think one won't hurt, or they want to drink so you figure one drink won't have too many carbs or something along those lines. A quick tip though; a lot of drinks do have carbs and on a Optavia diet, it is really not recommended because you'll bust straight through your numbers. Some people even give in to the peer pressure because their friends get upset that someone is not eating like the rest of them. When we eat more fat than we can absorb, our bodies just let it pass through us. This is largely harmless but has the side effect of damaging our gut bacteria, one of the exact things we are trying to fix without diet. So, if you notice these side effects, start reducing your fat intake until your stools return to normal.

Besides these symptoms, you should also experience a whole host of beneficial symptoms. Some of the most beneficial symptoms, like an improvement in metabolism, and weight loss, will take longer to happen. But others happen within days. You will find your appetite begins to come under your control. As your insulin spikes and crashes disappear, your body gets used to having a steady supply of energy. This means that rather than feeling hungry every single time your blood sugar drops, and snacking between meals, you are eating a healthy meal and going straight through to the next one without feeling hungry.

You will find that yeast infections and skin conditions improve, or even disappear entirely. This is because your candida is not being fed, so it has nothing to grow from. You can be at a dinner with a few friends and they want to share an appetizer and you think one won't hurt, or they want to drink so you figure one drink won't have too many carbs or something along those lines. A quick tip though; a lot of drinks do have carbs and on a Optavia diet, it is really not recommended because you'll bust straight through your numbers. Some people even give in to the peer pressure because their friends get upset that someone is not eating like the rest of them. Candida causes many types of yeast infection, and several types of skin problem, being the root cause of most cases of dandruff, for starters. It also makes other conditions, like eczema, worse, by irritating the skin and growing under and around dead skin cells.

You will find your moods are more even. That "hangry" feeling you get when your blood sugar drops is not normal. It is your body responding to a lack of glucose, trying to get you to eat carbs. At first you may feel the carb-hungry anger more intensely than usual, but after a couple of days your body gets used to not having those constant spikes and crashes in blood sugar. No energy crashes means no cravings, means no eating carbs, means no spikes, means no more crashes. It is vitally important to fight this cycle and restore order, even if you have no intention of following a Optavia diet for life.

How Weight Loss Is Achieved in General?

Before we look at the best way that you can use intermittent fasting to help you reduce your body fat percentage, let's first quickly consider how weight loss generally works – think of this as the science behind effective and guaranteed weight loss.

When you eat something – regardless of what it is – it means you are putting calories into your body. Nutrients are broken down and absorbed by your body, while carbohydrates are broken down and then processed into glucose, which is then distributed through your body to provide cells with energy.

When excess glucose is present in your body, it will usually be stored as fat cells through a rather complicated process that we are not going to be discussing in detail here. As fat cells increase, you gain weight – ultimately leading to you becoming overweight and then slowly obese.

Now, on the other hand, when you are physically active – whether you are walking, dancing, or going hard on the treadmill at the gym – you are burning calories. Your body uses more glucose for energy, and when the reserves run out, the body starts looking toward stored fat cells in order to generate more energy. This energy then allows you to continue running on that treadmill or allows you to pick up the set of weights a few more times.

So, to sum this up – you eat, you gain calories; you exercise, you lose calories.

When the number of calories you eat surpasses the number of calories you lose, then you gain weight. Think of this within a 24-hour cycle. If you eat 2,000 calories, but only burn 1,000, then you gain weight to the value of those extra 1,000 calories that are left behind at the end of the day.

When you eat more calories than you burn, it means there is a caloric surplus. You are gaining weight and cannot lose weight with this strategy.

To lose weight, this entire equation needs to be in an opposite manner. You need to lose more calories than you burn. If you eat food that calculates to around 2,000 calories each day, you need to burn more than the 2,000 calories if you wish ever to see your fat go away and the number of the scale go down.

When your daily calorie intake is less than the number of calories you lose, then it means you have a caloric deficit – this is the ideal goal that you are striving toward when you are aiming to reduce your body weight.

Weight Loss Through a Caloric Deficit

With intermittent fasting, you still need to create a caloric deficit. I've seen some people think that simply because they are fasting, they will lose weight, regardless of the other factors in their life. This is not true.

No matter how beneficial fasting might be and a program that utilizes intermittent fasting, you will still need to take the science behind weight loss into account. If your caloric intake is more than how many calories you lose in a day, then you set the way for weight gain and not weight loss.

Intermittent fasting can make things a little easier, however. It has been found that people who follow an intermittent fasting program eventually experience improvements in their level of satiety.

Their appetite is reduced, in other words. Since weight gain often lies within the fact that a person is unable to control their urges to eat inappropriate times, the reduced appetite will certainly be beneficial.

Additionally, because all meals of the day need to be squeezed into an eight-hour window with the particular intermittent fasting method that I am focusing on in this guide, it usually means that you will still feel somewhat full with your second meal after you had your first. When the time comes to have your third meal, the second meal will still be satisfying your appetite a little. You'll end up not wanting to overload your plate every chance you get – this means it becomes much, much easier than before to be in control of how many calories you will be consuming on a day-to-day basis.

Now, combine this with exercise. You won't even have to hit the gym too hard and may even be able to burn an adequate number of calories exercising at home if you are able to reduce the number of calories you consume by simply feeling full from the last meal when the time for the next meal comes.

Chapter 6: Potential Side Effects

Optavia meal plans are not appropriate for pregnant ladies. And individuals who engage in very common, excessive bodily hobby must avoid the five&1 application as it does now not deliver good enough energy or nutrients to support top-quality health.

And very low caloric consumption inclusive of 800-one thousand consistent with day can also reason adrenal stress, menstrual adjustments, compromised mental functioning, and we already explained it could have an impact on metabolic feature. (10, 11, 12, 13, 14)

Then you've got the reality that the prepackaged meals are processed that could cause digestive pain, specifically with the powdered protein.

So, side outcomes are possible for some humans but that's why it's vital to pick a plan maximum finest for you or skip out on the application altogether in case you recognize you cannot have positive ingredients.

Pros

1. Easy to follow

2. Convenient

3. Decent style of foods offered

4. One-on-one training and other assist

5. Can provide health advantages

The convenience is one very appealing function of Optavia plans (specially the five&1 or even the 4&2&1). You don't must prepare food because it's also portioned for you with the right quantity of energy. Plus, they provide a nice selection of fuelings so you're not likely to get bored with the meals.

The education and help is also something that many human beings opt for as they may be held accountable and can have any questions replied. Finally, there are many health blessings because of caloric and carbs restrict as discussed formerly.

But you want to have adequate nutrients and Optavia does provide entire food resources that are low-carbs. Although, the ingredients are decently processed and also, you'll want to decide if it's worth it long term. It's continually preferred to eat natural, minimally-processed meals sources.

Cons

* Pricey

* Fuelings are processed

* 5&1 may be too low in calories for some human beings

- Excessively low calories can result in weight regain
- Limited gluten-loose options
- No vegan alternatives
- Most coaches aren't fitness experts

Optavia virtually isn't cheap therefore it's not for every person. We already explained how the ingredients are processed to some extent and how too little energy can be unhealthy for some people or even likely purpose regain of weight due to slowing the metabolism inflicting the frame to burn fewer calories.

There also are restricted gluten-free and vegan alternatives no vegan plan as it is no longer advocated by using them that is a deal breaker for a few people and finally, maximum of the coaches aren't qualified to offer good sized fitness recommendation. But they're still amazing to have for aid and encouragement and it's usually recommended to do your personal due diligence as misinformation isn't uncommon.

However, with the unfastened assist, you will get right of entry to expert advice.

Chapter 7: What to Eat

On the entirety of Optavia's arrangements, both "fuelings" and "lean and green" custom made suppers are kept inside severe calorie ranges. Depending on the Optavia diet plan you select, you'll eat somewhere in the range of two to five of the companies pre-made supper substitutions ("fuelings") every day. You'll likewise plan and eat one to three of your own low-calorie meals, which ought to be principally lean protein and non-dull vegetables. Albeit no food is in fact prohibited on the eating regimen, many, (for example, desserts) are firmly disheartened. There are additionally a lot of nourishments that are strongly suggested, including healthy fats.

Notwithstanding lean protein and non-boring vegetables, a "lean and green" supper can be set up with up to two servings of sound fats, including olive or pecan oil, flaxseed, or avocado.

On Optavia's weight upkeep plans, clients can start to reintroduce other nutritional categories. Low-fat dairy, new organic product, and entire grains are totally remembered for Optavias 3 and 3 and 4 and 2 and 1 weight upkeep programs.

Resistant Foods

While Optavia's arrangements don't disallow explicit nourishments, they do exhort that you maintain a strategic distance from or limit your admission of less solid alternatives that aren't probably going to help your weight loss and don't offer significant sustenance.

Liberal Desserts

Of course, Optavia demoralizes reveling your sugar yearnings with desserts like cakes, treats, or frozen yogurt.

Nonetheless, after the underlying weight reduction stage, moderate sweet treats like new natural product or enhanced yogurt can advance go into your eating regimen.

Unhealthy Additions

Spread, shortening, and high-fat serving of mixed greens dressings include flavor, yet they likewise include a lot of calories. On Optavia, you'll be encouraged to downplay augmentations or substitute lower-calorie forms.

Sweet Beverages

Improved refreshments like pop, juice, or caffeinated drinks give calories absent a lot of satiation, so they're firmly debilitated on Optavia's arrangements.

Alcohol

The Optavia diet urges clients to restrict liquor. On the off chance that you're attempting to remain inside a severe calorie go, a 5-ounce glass of wine for 120 calories or the 150 calories in a 12-ounce brew will include quick.

Recommended Timing

On the off chance that you buy an Optavia Diet plan, you'll be furnished with a guide that offers proposals for when to eat each "energizing" meal.

When all is said and done, Optavia urges clients to eat about each a few hours.

For instance, a day of eating on the 5 and 1 program (included 5 "fuelings" and 1 natively constructed "lean and green" supper) could resemble this:

Breakfast: Fueling (1)

Early in the day nibble: Fueling (1)

Lunch: Fueling (1)

Evening nibble: Fueling (1)

Supper: Homemade "lean and green" meal

Night nibble: Fueling (1)

While a great many people decide to make supper their "lean and green" meal, Optavia stresses that it can any dinner of the day that works for you.

Optavia offers assets that layout best practices for setting up your "lean and green" meals.

The eating regimen doesn't require explicit plans yet takes note of that barbecuing, heating, poaching, and searing are the suggested cooking strategies for meats and other protein decisions.

In the event that you need some new supper thoughts, Optavia additionally keeps up a Pinterest leading group of plan-agreeable plans.

An extra asset that makes the Optavia program one of a kind is the accessibility of a mentor (normally an individual who has effectively finished the Optavia program) to root for you all through your weight reduction venture.

Modifications

The Optavia diet depends on exclusive meal substitution items and carefully calorie-controlled arranged suppers, so there's very little space for alteration.

The 5 & 1 arrangement limits calories to as low as 800-1000 every day, so it's not appropriate for individuals who are pregnant or take part in overwhelming activity.

Extraordinary calorie limitation can cause weakness, mind mist, cerebral pains, or menstrual changes. Accordingly, the 5 & 1 alternative ought not to be utilized for a long time.

In any case, the 3 & 3 and $ and 2 & 1 plans ordinarily gracefully between 1100 to 2500 calories for each day and can be proper to use for a more extended period.

Optavia Diet Effective

Caloric restriction is primes to weight reduction and the five&1 software is in particular conducive to shedding kilos rapid with an 800-one thousand calorie nutritional plan. Carbs also are stored low with a decent amount of protein per serving which is right for effective weight reduction in maximum instances.

Plus, carb and calorie restrict have shown to have many health advantages which includes advanced glucose metabolism, adjustments in frame composition, reduced danger of cardiovascular chance elements, and other disorder chance elements as nicely. (1)

But the 5&1 may not be for anyone as dropping weight too speedy and excessive calorie restrict can be damaging to your health and also you virtually won't experience excellent, at the same time as muscle loss is likewise a opportunity. 800-one thousand energy are quite low, in standard.

However, for weight loss, eating 800-1000 energy can be safe and effective if no longer applied for extended periods.

Research suggests that too few calories can have an effect on metabolism over the years that could motive you to regain misplaced weight. (three, four)

But this will additionally be due to long term habits as there are also several different variables to recall in terms of the differences among people. Weight loss isn't continually easy and retaining it off may be even more difficult however it requires everlasting life-style changes.

Optavia additionally recommends 30 minutes a day of exercise which is likewise important for maintaining weight off and maintaining proper health.

Research suggests that it's crucial to set sensible goals, on the subject of a character's needs, preferences, and contemporary health. Diets ought to be nutritionally ok for every man or woman which once more, may additionally vary. (5)

But scientific literature does, in reality, support using meal replacements as an powerful option for weight reduction and sort 2 diabetes. One take a look at of 119 individuals found that element-controlled meal replacements yielded considerably more weight reduction and upkeep of the load whilst in comparison to a general, self-decided on meals-primarily based weight loss program after 1 12 months. (6)

There was also a study that in comparison the Optavia five&1 weight loss program plus phone aid (OPT) to the decreased-calorie Medifast® 4&2&1 self-guided plan (MED), and also to a self-directed, decreased-calorie manage food plan. 198 individuals had been randomly assigned to both eating regimen for evaluation at some point of a 16-week period. (7)

Well, the OPT and MED businesses experienced considerably more weight reduction and belly fats than the self-directed control weight loss plan group. And it changed into concluded that the considerable weight reduction difference turned into corrclated with the meal replacements and make contact with aid.

Keep in thoughts even though, the look at turned into funded by Medifast. But there are numerous studies which have observed education help to be very effective for weight loss.

Whether it's sustainable and healthful long time, properly, there isn't sufficient proof for us to make that judgment.

However, the prepackaged meals from Optavia are processed to a degree so there are positive delivered elements along with meals components, and even processed oils that might not be healthful in huge quantities. Optavia is a clean label product so there are not any synthetic colorations, flavors, or sweeteners. Eight, nine

But it's best cautioned to get normal checkups and preferably, not continue to be on a program for too lengthy after you've lost the load. Although, they propose their three&3 plan when you've reached your weight so it's in the long run up to the man or woman as to whether or not or now not they need to hold with a application and training.

He defined in an Instagram put up that he was satisfied with the consequences despite the fact that this turned into lower back in 2018.

Also, U.S. News and World Report ranks Optavia #2 for great weight reduction diets, #10 for nice industrial food plan plans, although it ranks #27 for wholesome diets.

So once more, for weight loss, it could be an exceptional weight loss program software although for health, well, that's in which it could not be really worth it in the lengthy haul.

This is where Optavia claims to stand out among different diet programs and the training glaringly helps to maintain the clients advantageous and influenced which most probable leads to extra consistency.

The manual is also very beneficial as it offers you all the fundamentals so that you can effortlessly check with it at any time. Optavia also gives meal pointers and recipes via multiple social structures.

Program Costs

Optavia offers several different options but we've provided a tough fee of the basic programs.

5&1

For the 5&1 software, you get about 3 weeks' worth of fuelings and assist for a little over $400 and whilst you be a part of the Premier Club you'll get five loose packing containers for your first order and a blender bottle. You also have the choice to customize your food alternatives that's the equal for the opposite two packages as nicely.

Four&2&1

The 4&2&1 plan is a similar fee however while you join you get 20% off plus a blender bottle and 5 loose bins of fuelings.

Three & three

This plan is glaringly the cheapest and around $330 for 130 servings. You'll additionally get 5 free packing containers of fuelings and a blender bottle.

You need to additionally aspect in the food which you'll be cooking at domestic as properly and it can absolutely upload up for individuals who won't be capable of come up with the money for it lengthy-term. The gain right here and the purpose for the pricing is manifestly the ease and support you get. So, it could be well worth it to some humans.

Chapter 8: Overview Of The Optavia Recipes

In this chapter, we will focus on how this diet works and how your body transitions from one way of functioning to another.

As mentioned before, the Optavia diet was used mainly to lower the incidence of seizures in epileptic children.

As things usually go, people wanted to check out how the Optavia diet would work with an entirely healthy person.

This diet's primary purpose is to make your body switch from the way it used to function to an entirely new way of creating energy, keeping you healthy and alive.

How Optavia Works

Once you start following the Optavia diet, you will notice that things are changing, first and foremost, in your mind. Before, carbohydrates were your main body 'fuel' and were used to create glucose so that your brain could function. Now you no longer feed yourself with them.

In the beginning, most people feel odd because their usual food is off the table. When your menu consists of more fats and proteins, it is natural to feel that something is missing.

Your brain alarms you that you haven't eaten enough and sends you signals that you are hungry. It is literally "panicking" and telling you that you are starving, which is not correct. You get to eat, and you get to eat plenty of good food, but not carbs.

This condition usually arises during the first day or two. Afterward, people get used to their new eating habits.

Once the brain "realizes" that carbs are no longer an option, it will focus on "finding" another abundant energy source: in this case, fats.

Not only is your food rich in fats, but your body contains stored fats in large amounts. As you consume more fats and fewer carbs, your body "runs" on the fats, both consumed and stored. The best thing is that, as the fats are used for energy, they are burned. This is how you get a double gain from this diet.

Usually, it will take a few days of consuming low-carb meals before you start seeing visible weight loss results. In fact, you will not even have to check your weight because the fat layers will be visibly reduced.

This diet requires you to lower your daily consumption of carbs to only 20 grams. For most people, this transition from a regular carb-rich diet can be quite a challenge. Most people are used to eating bread, pasta, rice, dairy products, sweets, soda, alcohol, and fruits, so quitting all these foods might be a little challenging.

However, this is all in your head. If you manage to win the "battle" with your mind and endure the diet for a few days, you will see that as time goes by, you no longer have cravings at all. Plus, the weight loss and the fat burn will be a great motivation to continue with this diet.

The Optavia diet practically makes the body burn fats much faster than carbohydrates; the foods you consume with this diet are quite rich in fats. Carbs will be there, too but at far lower levels than before. Foods rich in carbohydrates are the body's primary fuel or the brain's food. (Our bodies turn carbs into glucose.) Because there are hardly any carbohydrates in this diet, the body will have to find a substitute source of energy to keep itself alive.

Many people who don't truly need to lose weight and who are completely healthy still choose to follow the Optavia diet because it is a great way to keep their meals balanced. Also, it is the perfect way to cleanse the body of toxins, processed foods, sugars, and unnecessary carbs. The combination of these things is usually the main reason for heart failure, some cancers, diabetes, cholesterol, or obesity.

If you ask a nutritionist about this diet, they will recommend it without a doubt. So, if you feel like cleansing your body and starting a diet that will keep you healthy, well-fed, and slender, perhaps the Optavia diet should be your primary choice.

And what is the best thing about it (besides the fact that you will balance your weight and lower the risk of many diseases)?

There is no yo-yo effect. The Optavia diet can be followed forever and has no side effects. It does not restrict you to following it for a few weeks or a month. Once you get your body used to Optavia foods, you will not think about going back to the old ways of eating your meals.

Chapter 9: Optavia Phases

Your diet is now rich in fats, which become the main energy supply for your body.

Many people wonder whether they will be able to know when they have entered the state of Optavia. The answer is yes.

As the Optaviane levels in your blood increase, and as your body turns towards fats as an energy source, they will start providing you with energy. They will burn at the same time, which means you will start losing weight. The changes will be visible because the fat layers will start disappearing in front of your eyes.

Your carbohydrate intake should not be over 20 grams per day. However, this will not be a challenge because the diet offers many delicious replacements for bread, sweets, snacks, pizza, and pasta.

Another thing that is limited in this diet is protein intake. Increased protein intake will not help you get in the state of Optavia. Rather, it will have the opposite effect. This is why the Optavia diet limits protein intake (0.6-0.8 grams per kilogram of body mass; so, for a body weight of about 55-56kg/123 pounds, you need to limit your protein intake to 78-79 grams).

After a day or two of Optavia meals, your body will increase the Optavia bodies in your blood. This is achieved when carbs are reduced, but also with intermittent fasting (which should not be done immediately, if you haven't fasted before).

To ensure that your body is in a state of Optavia, you can get a blood test, but if you don't want to do that, you will notice some symptoms such as:

- Stinky breath – Yes, it's not the coolest thing, but this is one of the first symptoms. It's not like your breath will smell terrible, but you will notice that your breath has a fruity odor that occurs when one follows any diet (Paleo, for example). This is nothing that can't be fixed by brushing your teeth or chewing mint gum.

- Dehydration – The state of Optavia might make you feel thirstier than usual. Don't hesitate to drink enough water while you are following this diet. Water will improve your digestion, help you feel full, and, of course, help you get rid of your bad breath (besides mints and toothpaste).

- Frequent urination – Optavia bodies are a natural diuretic, so no matter how much water you drink, you will feel the need to visit the bathroom more often than before.

- Optavia bodies in your blood – If you want to be certain that you are in the state of Optavia, you can have a blood test done. Your doctor will tell you exactly how many Optavia bodies are in your blood. The increased number means that you have entered Optavia and that the diet is working well.

- Feeling sleepy – Don't worry if you feel tired. It is normal because suddenly you have changed your diet and your body is trying to adjust to the new energy sources. Carbs are known to give you energy, so until your body learns that it has a new energy source, you might feel a bit tired. Make sure you get enough sleep and rest.

- Headaches – Most people who start following this diet feel mild headaches. Usually, they go away within a day, but there have been cases in which the headaches lasted for about a week. This indicator should not worry you; your body is not getting the usual amount of carbs and sugars. (The Octavia diet limits the intake of sugars such as chocolate, juices, soda, cakes, and some fruits.) In addition, the headaches might occur due to dehydration or an imbalance of electrolytes. If the headaches last for longer than a week, please see your doctor.

Optavia Diet Tips and Tricks for Success

Manage your hunger properly: When they are first adapting to the Optavia diet, one of the most frequent problems that many people have is that they don't plan ahead for situations where they know they are likely to get hungry before they can easily find access to another Optavia meal. This type of situation is extremely easy to prepare for, especially if you already have some fat bombs on hand, or you can even experiment with premade Optavia options. The important thing is that you prevent yourself from getting so hungry that you are overly concerned with filling the hole in your stomach and not nearly concerned enough with filling your void with nutritious alternatives. Additionally, you will want to ensure that you try and eat at the same time each day to help your body learn when to expect its next meal.

This will be especially important for when you exercise as you will want to eat some healthy fats beforehand to ensure you have the energy to give it your all. When you are finished, you will want to be sure to follow it up with protein to help your muscles get the most from the experience as possible. If you find yourself ending up too hungry after you exercise, keep in mind that a long, mild, workout is just as effective as a short, intense, workout and much less demanding on the body. Stretch things out, and you will likely find that you have less of an urge to binge after you are finished.

Shirataki noodles are your friend: While you might not have heard of the shirataki noodle yet, if you plan on sticking to the Optavia diet for a prolonged period of time it will soon be your best friend. Also known as the miracle noodle, shirataki noodles are made from the konjac plant and then formed into either noodles or rice. Shirataki noodles have one net gram of carbs per 100 grams of noodles which is far more than you will consume in an average serving. While they aren't nutritious, they are a good source of fiber and is a great way to make a wide variety of non-Optavia dishes Optavia without having to change anything else about them.

In addition to this major benefit, studies show that the type of fiber found in the shirataki noodle, known as glucomannan, has numerous different benefits on its own. First, it is proven to decrease feelings of hunger more effectively than other types of fiber which means that eating it as part of a meal will naturally make it easier for you to eat healthy portion sizes. Additionally, it is known to decrease several of the risk factors for heart disease including fasting blood sugar, cholesterol, triglycerides and LDL cholesterol. If you have issues with overeating, it will also help your body to only absorb an appropriate amount of the fat, protein and carbs that you consume.

It is not without potential issues to be aware of, however. First and foremost, as it is known to expand up to 50 times in water, it can cause digestive issues including mild diarrhea, gas and bloating in some people who eat it. It is also known to reduce the overall bioavailability of some oral medications and supplements which means you will want to speak a doctor before adding it as a regular part of your diet if you feel this may concern you. Additionally, this response only occurs in a small fraction of the population which means that it is definitely worth trying and seeing how you like it.

Know your exact net carb limit: While you will want to stick to 15 or less net carbs per day when first entering Optaviasis, this is just to save you the hassle of determining the exact amount of net carbs that your body can handle. The fact of the matter is that each person will have a different net carb limit, which can also change over time. To provide yourself with all the data you need to ensure that you have an accurate idea of just what is going on.

One of the most popular ways of doing so these days is through the use of the MyFitnessPal app which is one of the most popular calorie tracking apps around today, and with good reason. The base version is free, though some of the paid features are useful to those who are following the Optavia diet. The app also sets itself apart with the ease at which it is to share the progress. The app has a very large food database, but anyone can edit it, so it can sometimes be difficult to tell if the macros are reliable. Finally, the free version only tracks regular carbs, plus fiber so you will have to do a little math as well.

If you are looking for something that is tailored to the Optavia diet specifically, then you may be interested in Chronometer. While it costs $2.99, it comes with an officially curated food database which provides far more details about the foods you are considering putting into your body in addition to natively calculating Optavia macros.

Being able to precisely track what you are eating comes with numerous benefits on its own as well. First and foremost, you will find that you can exert willpower over what you are eating much more easily when you know you have to account for it specifically. Additionally, it will help you to get a more accurate picture of what you are consuming during the day as you will be surprised at how many small things you eat during the day that you don't think of as either eating a meal or snacking. Finally, it will help to ensure that you get in the habit of measuring the foods you eat until you have an accurate idea of what a true serving size is.

When done properly, watching your net carbs closely will make it possible to slowly ramp up the number of net carbs you can consume in a day without putting your Optavia state at risk. While this may seem cumbersome and restrictive at first, it should be an easy habit to get into, and the end result will be more carbs, and thus more options, in your diet which will more than make up for the early hassle.

Be aware of Optavia: Optavia is a deadly combination of overly high Optavia levels, metabolic acidosis, and hyperglycemia that kills around 5,000 people per year, a vast majority of those are people who were already dealing with complications as a result of diabetes. If you are not one the roughly 400 million people worldwide who are dealing with some type of diabetes, then the odds of you contracting this condition are negligible. You would have to put yourself through the type of years of poor eating, lack of exercise and extreme stress that causes type 2 diabetes before your odds of contracting Optavia began to increase.

For those who are dealing with diabetes, the Optavia diet is still quite safe, as long as they are actively dealing with any issues that may cause them to end up with an untreated insulin deficiency. Optavia often occurs quite quickly, in as little as 24 hours. Symptoms include vomiting and abdominal pain, in addition to an increased heart rate, high blood glucose levels, and low blood pressure. The person suffering from Optavia will also start off alert and slowly become more and more drowsy as the condition worsens.

Remaining in Optaviasis while eating out: While planning ahead is the easiest way to ensure that eating at a restaurant like a normal human being isn't an overly complicated disaster, sometimes the unexpected happens, and you will find yourself with no choice but to face a menu unprepared. Keep the following rules in mind, and you will be able to make it through with your Optavianes intact.

First and foremost, you will want to stick to the basics. If you are at a fast food restaurant, then you will want to avoid anything that is likely to have had sugar added to it, which admittedly will be most of the menu. Nevertheless, you should be able to power through with some type of non-breaded meat, either plain or with cheese. While you may think you will be able to get away with a salad, even non-fast food restaurants typically fill their salads with light, leafy greens and berries, all of which are quite high in carbs. If you will get a salad, ensure it includes plenty of meat and that any dressing only comes on the side.

In general, whatever you order you will want to ensure that it is free of sauces or dressings as it can be very difficult to determine with any degree of certainty what is actually in them. In general, you can trust fattier salad dressings, in moderation, such as blue cheese, Caesar, and ranch. Even better, if possible simply ask for a side of butter.

If you aren't sure about finding something on the menu that works for you, don't be afraid to try a special request. While lower-tier restaurants may not always be able to meet your needs, it certainly never hurts to try, after all, you are a paying customer. At the end of the day, if you aren't 100 percent sure about a given dish, it is better to go without as opposed to risking 20 or more net carbs on a single meal. While sometimes you will simply have no choice, generally it will be easier to skip a single meal than to work to get your body back into Optavia.

Sticking to the diet while traveling: While traveling can make remaining in a state of Optavia more challenging, once again it is more a matter of planning ahead than anything else. If you ever put off dealing with the food issue until the last minute, then you will have a more difficult time of it, guaranteed.

When traveling, the first thing you will want to do is to find a hotel that includes a kitchenette. This will make the entire process much more manageable, and with a quick trip to a local grocery store, you can have some of your favorites on hand at all times to ensure you aren't tempted into doing something that you will regret later on. The best part is that these types of special accommodations rarely cost much more than a more traditional room would as well. Just make sure you call ahead and ensure you have everything that you require from a kitchenette, as what qualifies can vary by location.

Beyond that, planning for your daily meals shouldn't be all that more difficult than when you plan for such things at home. All it really takes is a little legwork on a popular search engine as wherever you go there is likely an active Optavia community that can tell you all of the best restaurants and dishes to try regardless of your personal preferences. The biggest thing to keep in mind here is not to let the fact that you are on vacation justify eating poorly. While it might be a thrill to eat a week's worth of carbs in a day, you will most certainly regret it in the morning. Don't make that mistake, stay strong, you will be glad you did in the long run.

Eating Optavia on the cheap: While switching to a Optavia diet will likely leave you feeling better than you have in years, it can also be costlier, simply because of the fact that foods that are loaded with carbs are also often cheaper than the alternative. Luckily, it is perfectly possible to remain Optavia without breaking the bank. To get started, the first thing you will want to do is shop normally for a month or so to get a feel for the types of products you are most likely going to want to see more of.

While niche markets such as Whole Foods and Traders Joes will offer up plenty of products targeted at your demographic, if you are looking to save money then you will want to avoid these places like the plague. For starters, you will want to get a membership to a big box store like Costco or Sam's Club. These places routinely sell large cuts of meat for pennies on the dollar. What you don't use right away you can store, just be sure to go through the proper steps and use some type of vacuum sealer for the best results. You will also want to be sure that you mark everything with the date that you stored it to ensure that you rotate your stock regularly.

Additionally, when shopping you will want to focus on the core components of your meals, not purchasing pre-made meals, regardless of whether they are Optavia or not. The cost of buying a pre-made meal is often at least a third higher than buying all of the ingredients separately. While you will almost certainly need more time to eat Optavia, the results are more than worth it.

What Are The Benefits Of 5 Ingredients Optavia Diet Especially When Using Instant Pot?

Without overemphasis, there are numerous benefits associated with the use of 5 ingredients. These benefits range from time and energy management to health benefits.

Convenience: With the preset smart programs such as Rice, Congee/Porridge, Steaming, Slow Cook, Soup, Meat & Stew, Multigrain, Keep warm, Sauté/Browning, Yogurt, with Ferment, Pasteurize, and Jiu Niang-making settings featured in the instant pots, you are only few clicks away from making a super delicious meal for yourself.

Time Saving: Cooking at high pressure simply means cooking in a superheated medium. This superheated cooking medium makes it possible to cook food faster than necessary. A food that takes hour to be cooked in an ordinary cooking pot can be cooked within few minutes in an instant pot.

Elimination of Toxins and Harmful Microorganisms: Cooking food at high pressure helps a lot in the maintenance and promotion of good health. If you are a devotee of Lectin-free diet, then instant pot pressure cooker is a must have for you for easy cooking. Pressure cooking helps to eliminate some toxins, such as lectins and aflatoxin, from our meal. Also, cooking at temperature higher than 100°C exposes and destroys some harmful microorganisms that are resistant to temperature below 100°C.

Retention of Nutrients: Do you know that water-soluble nutrients are liable to escape our cooking pot through evaporation? Also, do you know that heat-sensitive nutrients can be easily destroyed as a result of prolonged exposure to heat? Yes, it happens and the best means to curb this loss is to prevent the evaporation of steam, cooking food as quick as possible, and heating all parts of the food evenly. With your instant pot in your kitchen, you have no cause to worry about loss if food nutrients.

Energy Efficiency: Here we are not talking about the energy from your body system. We know quite well that you can save yourself a lot of energy by using instant pot pressure cooker. So close your eyes and get one if don't have one already, and save yourself the stress of cooking with ordinary pots. The energy efficiency we are talking about here is the energy consumed by the pot itself during the cooking process. Survey has revealed that instant pot has the potential to save up to 70% energy when compared with other cooking vessels. With instant pot, you don't need too much liquid to cook your food ax you need it in other cooking methods. With less water, boiling is achieved faster. Another factor that leads to higher energy efficiency is the lagging feature of the pot. In instant pot, heat is not lost like you lose it in other cooking methods because instant pot is well insulated against heat loss. As a result, internal temperature of the cooking vessel goes up leading to reduced cooking time.

Chapter 10: First Courses And Soups

Tomato Braised Cauliflower with Chicken

Preparation Time: 15 minutes

Cooking Time: 30 minutes

Servings: 1

INGREDIENTS:

- 1 garlic clove, sliced
- 3/4 scallions, to be trimmed and cut into 1-inch pieces
- 1/8 teaspoon dried oregano
- 1/8 teaspoon red pepper flakes
- 1/4 cups cauliflower
- 3/4 cups diced canned tomatoes
- 1/4 cup fresh basil, gently torn
- 1/8 teaspoon each of pepper and salt, divided
- 3/4 teaspoon olive oil
- 3/4 pound boneless, skinless chicken breasts

DIRECTIONS:

1. Get a saucepan and combine the garlic, scallions, oregano, crushed red pepper, cauliflower, tomato, and add ¼ cup of water. Get everything boil together and add ¼ teaspoon of pepper and salt for seasoning, then cover the pot with a lid. Let it simmer for 10 minutes and stir as often as possible until you observe that the cauliflower is tender. Now, wrap up the seasoning with the remaining ¼ teaspoon of pepper and salt.

2. Using olive oil, toss the chicken breast and let it roast in the oven with the heat of 4500F for 20 minutes and an internal temperature of 1650F. Allow the chicken to rest for like 10 minutes.

3. Now slice the chicken and serve on a bed of tomato-braised cauliflower.

NUTRITION:

- **Calories:** 290
- **Fats:** 10g
- **Carbohydrates:** 13g
- **Protein:** 38g

Cheeseburger Soup

Preparation Time: 15 minutes

Cooking Time: 30 minutes

Servings: 1

INGREDIENTS:

- 1/16 cup chopped onion
- 1 quantity of (14.5 oz) can dice tomato
- 1/4 pound 90% lean ground beef
- 3/16 cup chopped celery
- 1/4 teaspoons Worcestershire sauce

- 1/2 cup chicken broth

- 1/8 teaspoon salt

- 1/4 teaspoon dried parsley

- 2/3 cups of baby spinach

- 1/8 teaspoon ground pepper

- 1 oz. reduced-fat shredded cheddar cheese

DIRECTIONS:

1. Get a large soup pot and cook the beef until it becomes brown. Add the celery, onion, and sauté until it becomes tender. Make sure to drain the excess liquid.

2. Stir in the broth, tomatoes, parsley, Worcestershire sauce, pepper, and salt. Cover and wait for it to simmer on low heat for about 20 minutes.

3. Add spinach and leave it to cook until it becomes wilted in about 1–3 minutes. Top each of your servings with 1 oz. of cheese.

NUTRITION:

- **Calories:** 400

- **Carbohydrates:** 11g

- **Protein:** 44g

- **Fats:** 20g

Tomatillo and Green Chili Pork Stew

Preparation Time: 15 minutes

Cooking Time: 30 minutes

Servings: 1

INGREDIENTS:

- 1/2 scallions, chopped

- 1/4 pound of boneless pork loin, to be cut into bite-sized cubes
- 1/2 cloves of garlic
- 1/4 pound tomatillos, trimmed and chopped
- 1/2 serrano chilies, seeds, and membranes
- ¼ cup coriander, chopped
- ¼ tablespoon (each) salt and paper
- 1/4 jalapeno, seeds, and membranes to be removed and thinly sliced
- 1/4 cup sliced radishes
- 1 lime wedge

DIRECTIONS:

1. Combine scallions, garlic, tomatillos, four lettuce leaves, serrano chilies, and oregano in a blender. Then puree until smooth.

2. Put pork and tomatillo mixture in a medium pot. 1-inch of puree should cover the pork; if not, add water until it covers it. Season with pepper & salt, and cover it simmers. For 20 minutes, let it simmer on low heat.

3. Now, finely shred the remaining lettuce leaves.

4. When the stew is done cooking, garnish with coriander, radishes, finely shredded lettuce, sliced jalapenos, and lime wedges.

NUTRITION:

- **Calories:** 370
- **Protein:** 36g
- **Carbohydrates:** 14g
- **Fats:** 19g

Rosemary Cauliflower Rolls

Preparation Time: 15 minutes

Cooking Time: 30 minutes

Servings: 1 (3 biscuits per serving)

INGREDIENTS:

- 1/12 cup almond flour
- 1 cup grated cauliflower
- 1/12 cup reduced-fat, shredded mozzarella, or cheddar cheese
- 1/2 eggs
- 1/2 tablespoons fresh rosemary, finely chopped
- ½ teaspoon salt

DIRECTIONS:

1. Preheat your oven to 4000F.
2. Pour all the ingredients in a medium-sized bowl.
3. Scoop cauliflower mixture into 12 evenly sized rolls/biscuits onto a lightly greased and foil-lined baking sheet.
4. Bake until it turns golden brown, which should be achieved in about 30 minutes.
5. Note: if you want to have the outside of the rolls/biscuits crisp, then broil for some minutes before serving.

NUTRITION:

- **Calories:** 138
- **Protein:** 11g
- **Carbohydrates:** 8g
- **Fats:** 7g

Braised Collard Beans in Peanut Sauce with Pork Tenderloin

Preparation Time: 25 minutes

Cooking Time: 35 minutes

Servings: 1

INGREDIENTS:

- 1/2 cups chicken stock
- 3 cups chopped collard greens
- 1 1/2 tablespoons powdered peanut butter
- 3/4 cloves of garlic, crushed
- 1/4 teaspoon salt
- 1/8 teaspoon allspice
- 1/8 teaspoon black pepper
- 1/2 teaspoons lemon juice
- 3/8 teaspoon hot sauce
- 1/8 pound pork tenderloin

DIRECTIONS:

1. Get a pot with a tight-fitting lid and combine the collards with the garlic, chicken stock, hot sauce, and half of the pepper and salt. Cook on low heat for about 1 hour or until the collards become tender.

2. Once the collards are tender, stir in the allspice, lemon juice. And they have powdered peanut butter. Keep warm.

3. Season the pork tenderloin with the remaining pepper and salt, and broil in a toaster oven for 10 minutes when you have an internal temperature of 1450F. Make sure to turn the tenderloin every 2 minutes to achieve an even browning all over. After that, you can take away the pork from the oven and allow it to rest for like 5 minutes.

4. Slice the pork as you will like and serve it on top of the braised greens.

NUTRITION:

- **Calories:** 320
- **Fats:** 10g

- **Carbohydrates:** 15g
- **Protein:** 45g

Tofu Power Bowl

Preparation Time: 10 minutes

Cooking Time: 15–20 minutes

Servings: 1

INGREDIENTS:

- 15 oz. extra-firm tofu
- 1 teaspoon rice vinegar
- 2 tablespoons soy sauce
- 1 teaspoon sesame oil
- ½ cup grated cauliflower
- ½ cup grated eggplant
- ½ cup chopped kale

DIRECTIONS:

1. Press tofu. Place another of clean dish towels or paper towels on top of the tofu.

2. Combine both the vinegar and soy sauce in a small bowl and whisk together.

3. Get a large skillet and heat the sesame oil in it. Place cubed tofu to cover one half of the skillet, and the cubed eggplant should cover the other half. Cook both together until they become slightly brown and tender in about 10–12 minutes. Remove from skillet and keep aside. Now, add kale and sauté until they become wilted in about 3–5 minutes.

4. Microwave the already grated cauliflower in a small bowl with one teaspoon of water for about 3–4 minutes until it becomes tender. **NUTRITION:**

- **Calories:** 117
- **Protein:** 14g
- **Carbohydrates:** 2.2g
- **Fats:** 7g

Grilled Veggie Kabobs

Preparation Time: 15 minutes

Cooking Time: 12 to 15 minutes

Servings: 1

INGREDIENTS:

Marinade:

- ½ cup balsamic vinegar
- 1/3 tablespoons minced thyme
- 1/4 tablespoons minced rosemary
- 1/2 cloves garlic, peeled and minced
- Sea salt, to taste (optional)
- Freshly ground black pepper, to taste

Veggies:

- 1/3 cups cherry tomatoes
- 1/3 red bell pepper, it should be seeded and cut into 1-inch pieces
- 1/3 green bell pepper, without seeds and cut into 1-inch pieces
- 1/3 medium yellow squash, cut into 1-inch rounds
- 1/3 medium zucchini, cut into 1-inch rounds
- 1/3 medium red onion skinned and cut into large chunks

Special Equipment:

- Two bamboo skewers, make sure to soak it in water for 30 minutes

DIRECTIONS:

1. Preheat the grill to medium heat.
2. In making the marinade: In a small bowl, stir together the balsamic vinegar, thyme, rosemary, garlic, salt (if desired), and pepper.

3. Thread veggies onto skewers, alternating between different-colored veggies.

4. Grill the veggies for 12 to 15 minutes until softened and lightly charred, brushing the veggies with the marinade and flipping the skewers every 4 to 5 minutes.

5. Remove from the grill and serve hot.

NUTRITION:

- **Calories:** 98
- **Fat:** 0.7g
- **Carbs:** 19.2g
- **Protein:** 3.8g
- **Fiber:** 3.4g

Chapter 11: Brunch & Dinner

Basil Tomato Frittata

Preparation Time: 10 minutes

Cooking Time: 15 minutes

Serve: 2

Ingredients:

- 5 eggs
- 1 tbsp olive oil
- 7 oz can artichokes
- 1 garlic clove, chopped
- 1 onion, chopped
- 1/2 cup cherry tomatoes
- 2 tbsp fresh basil, chopped
- 1/4 cup feta cheese, crumbled
- 1/4 tsp pepper
- 1/4 tsp salt

Directions:

1. Heat oil in a pan over medium heat.

2. Add garlic and onion and sauté for 4 minutes.
3. Add artichokes, basil, and tomatoes and cook for 4 minutes.
4. Beat eggs in a bowl and season with pepper and salt.
5. Pour egg mixture into the pan and cook for 5-7 minutes.
6. Serve and enjoy.

NUTRITION:

- Calories 325
- Fat 22 g
- Carbohydrates 14 g
- Sugar 6.2 g
- Protein 20 g
- Cholesterol 425 mg

Coconut Bread

Preparation Time: 10 minutes

Cooking Time: 35 minutes

Serve: 12

Ingredients:

- 6 eggs
- 1 tbsp baking powder
- 2 tbsp swerve
- 1/2 cup ground flaxseed
- 1/2 cup coconut flour
- 1/2 tsp cinnamon
- 1 tsp xanthan gum
- 1/3 cup unsweetened coconut milk
- 1/2 cup olive oil

- 1/2 tsp salt

Directions:

1. Preheat the oven to 375 F.
2. Add eggs, milk, and oil into the stand mixer and blend until combined.
3. Add remaining ingredients and blend until well mixed.
4. Pour batter in greased loaf pan.
5. Bake in oven for 40 minutes.
6. Slice and serve.

NUTRITION:

- Calories 150
- Fat 13.7 g
- Carbohydrates 6 g
- Sugar 3 g
- Protein 3.9 g
- Cholesterol 82 mg

Chia Spinach Pancakes

Preparation Time: 10 minutes

Cooking Time: 5 minutes

Serve: 6

Ingredients:

- 4 eggs
- ½ cup coconut flour
- 1 cup coconut milk
- ¼ cup chia seeds
- 1 cup spinach, chopped

- 1 tsp baking soda
- ½ tsp pepper
- ½ tsp salt

Directions:

1. Whisk eggs in a bowl until frothy.
2. Combine together all dry ingredients and add in egg mixture and whisk until smooth. Add spinach and stir well.
3. Greased pan with butter and heat over medium heat.
4. Pour 3-4 tablespoons of batter onto the pan and make pancake.
5. Cook pancake until lightly golden brown from both the sides.
6. Serve and enjoy.

NUTRITION:

- Calories 111
- Fat 7.2 g
- Carbohydrates 6 g
- Sugar 0.4 g
- Protein 6.3 g
- Cholesterol 110 mg

Olive Cheese Omelet

Preparation Time: 10 minutes

Cooking Time: 5 minutes

Serve: 4

Ingredients:

- 4 large eggs
- 2 oz cheese

- 12 olives, pitted
- 2 tbsp butter
- 2 tbsp olive oil
- 1 tsp herb de Provence
- 1/2 tsp salt

Directions:

1. Add all ingredients except butter in a bowl whisk well until frothy.
2. Melt butter in a pan over medium heat.
3. Pour egg mixture onto hot pan and spread evenly.
4. Cover and cook for 3 minutes.
5. Turn omelet to other side and cook for 2 minutes more.
6. Serve and enjoy.

NUTRITION:

- Calories 250
- Fat 23 g
- Carbohydrates 2 g
- Sugar 1 g
- Protein 10 g
- Cholesterol 216 mg

Feta Kale Frittata

Preparation Time: 10 minutes

Cooking Time: 2 Hour 10 minutes

Serve: 8

Ingredients:

- 8 eggs, beaten

- 4 oz feta cheese, crumbled
- 6 oz bell pepper, roasted and diced
- 5 oz baby kale
- 1/4 cup green onion, sliced
- 2 tsp olive oil

Directions:

1. Heat olive oil in a pan over medium-high heat.
2. Add kale to the pan and sauté for 4-5 minutes or until softened.
3. Spray slow cooker with cooking spray.
4. Add cooked kale into the slow cooker.
5. Add green onion and bell pepper into the slow cooker.
6. Pour beaten eggs into the slow cooker and stir well to combine.
7. Sprinkle crumbled feta cheese.
8. Cook on low for 2 hours or until frittata is set.
9. Serve and enjoy.

NUTRITION:

- Calories 150
- Fat 9 g
- Carbohydrates 10 g
- Sugar 5 g
- Protein 10 g
- Cholesterol 175 mg

Blueberry Muffins

Preparation Time: 10 minutes

Cooking Time: 25 minutes

Serve: 12

Ingredients:

- 2 eggs
- ½ tsp vanilla
- 1/2 cup fresh blueberries
- 1 tsp baking powder
- 6 drops stevia
- 1 cup heavy cream
- 2 cups almond flour
- 1/4 cup butter, melted

Directions:

1. Preheat the oven to 350 F.
2. Add eggs to the mixing bowl and whisk until well mix.
3. Add remaining ingredients to the eggs and mix well to combine.
4. Pour batter into greased muffin tray and bake in oven for 25 minutes.
5. Serve and enjoy.

NUTRITION:

- Calories 190
- Fat 18 g
- Carbohydrates 6 g
- Sugar 1.4 g
- Protein 5.4 g
- Cholesterol 55 mg

Cheese Zucchini Eggplant

Preparation Time: 10 minutes

Cooking Time: 2 hours

Serve: 8

Ingredients:

- 1 eggplant, peeled and cut in 1-inch cubes
- 1 ½ cup spaghetti sauce
- 1 onion, sliced
- 1 medium zucchini, cut into 1-inch pieces
- 1/2 cup parmesan cheese, shredded

Directions:

1. Add all ingredients into the crock pot and stir well.
2. Cover and cook on high for 2 hours.
3. Stir well and serve.

NUTRITION:

- Calories 47
- Fat 1.2 g
- Carbohydrates 8 g
- Sugar 4 g
- Protein 2.5 g
- Cholesterol 2 mg

Broccoli Nuggets

Preparation Time: 10 minutes

Cooking Time: 15 minutes

Serve: 4

Ingredients:

- 2 egg whites
- 2 cups broccoli florets
- 1/4 cup almond flour
- 1 cup cheddar cheese, shredded
- 1/8 tsp salt

Directions:

1. Preheat the oven to 350 F.
2. Add broccoli in bowl and mash using masher.
3. Add remaining ingredients to the broccoli and mix well.
4. Drop 20 scoops onto baking tray and press lightly down.
5. Bake in preheated oven for 20 minutes.
6. Serve and enjoy.

NUTRITION:

- Calories 145
- Fat 10.4 g
- Carbohydrates 4 g
- Sugar 1.1 g
- Protein 10.5 g
- Cholesterol 30 mg

Cauliflower Frittata

Preparation Time: 10 minutes

Cooking Time: 5 minutes

Serve: 1

Ingredients:

- 1 egg
- 1/2 tbsp onion, diced
- ¼ cup cauliflower rice
- 1 tbsp olive oil
- 1/4 tsp turmeric
- Pepper
- Salt

Directions:

1. Add all ingredients except oil into the bowl and mix well to combine.
2. Heat oil in a pan over medium heat.
3. Pour the mixture into the hot oil pan and cook for 3-4 minutes or until lightly golden brown.
4. Serve and enjoy.

NUTRITION:

- Calories 196
- Fat 19 g
- Carbohydrates 3 g
- Sugar 1 g
- Protein 7 g
- Cholesterol 165 mg

Coconut Kale Muffins

Preparation Time: 10 minutes

Cooking Time: 30 minutes

Serve: 8

Ingredients:

- 6 eggs
- 1/2 cup unsweetened coconut milk
- 1 cup kale, chopped
- ¼ tsp garlic powder
- ¼ tsp paprika
- 1/4 cup green onion, chopped
- Pepper
- Salt

Directions:

1. Preheat the oven to 350 F.
2. Add all ingredients into the bowl and whisk well.
3. Pour mixture into the greased muffin tray and bake in oven for 30 minutes.
4. Serve and enjoy.

NUTRITION:

- Calories 92
- Fat 7 g
- Carbohydrates 2 g
- Sugar 0.8 g
- Protein 5 g
- Cholesterol 140 mg

Protein Muffins

Preparation Time: 10 minutes

Cooking Time: 15 minutes

Serve: 12

Ingredients:

- 8 eggs
- 2 scoop vanilla protein powder
- 8 oz cream cheese
- 4 tbsp butter, melted

Directions:

1. In a large bowl, combine together cream cheese and melted butter.
2. Add eggs and protein powder and whisk until well combined.
3. Pour batter into the greased muffin pan.
4. Bake at 350 F for 25 minutes.
5. Serve and enjoy.

NUTRITION:

- Calories 149
- Fat 12 g
- Carbohydrates 2 g
- Sugar 0.4 g
- Protein 8 g
- Cholesterol 115 mg

Healthy Waffles

Preparation Time: 10 minutes

Cooking Time: 10 minutes

Serve: 4

Ingredients:

- 8 drops liquid stevia
- 1/2 tsp baking soda
- 1 tbsp chia seeds
- 1/4 cup water
- 2 tbsp sunflower seed butter
- 1 tsp cinnamon
- 1 avocado, peel, pitted and mashed
- 1 tsp vanilla
- 1 tbsp lemon juice
- 3 tbsp coconut flour

Directions:

1. Preheat the waffle iron.
2. In a small bowl, add water and chia seeds and soak for 5 minutes.
3. Mash together sunflower seed butter, lemon juice, vanilla, stevia, chia mixture, and avocado.
4. Mix together cinnamon, baking soda, and coconut flour.
5. Add wet ingredients to the dry ingredients and mix well.
6. Pour waffle mixture into the hot waffle iron and cook on each side for 3-5 minutes.
7. Serve and enjoy.

NUTRITION:

- Calories 220
- Fat 17 g

- Carbohydrates 13 g
- Sugar 1.2 g
- Protein 5.1 g
- Cholesterol 0 mg

Cheese Almond Pancakes

Preparation Time: 10 minutes

Cooking Time: 10 minutes

Serve: 4

Ingredients:

- 4 eggs
- 1/4 tsp cinnamon
- 1/2 cup cream cheese
- 1/2 cup almond flour
- 1 tbsp butter, melted

Directions:

1. Add all ingredients into the blender and blend until combined.
2. Melt butter in a pan over medium heat.
3. Pour 3 tablespoons of batter per pancake and cook for 2 minutes on each side.
4. Serve and enjoy.

NUTRITION:

- Calories 271
- Fat 25 g
- Carbohydrates 5 g
- Sugar 1 g
- Protein 10.8 g

- Cholesterol 203 mg

Vegetable Quiche

Preparation Time: 10 minutes

Cooking Time: 30 minutes

Serve: 6

Ingredients:

- 8 eggs
- 1 onion, chopped
- 1 cup Parmesan cheese, grated
- 1 cup unsweetened coconut milk
- 1 cup tomatoes, chopped
- 1 cup zucchini, chopped
- 1 tbsp butter
- 1/2 tsp pepper
- 1 tsp salt

Directions:

1. Preheat the oven to 400 F.
2. Melt butter in a pan over medium heat then add onion and sauté until onion soften.
3. Add tomatoes and zucchini to pan and sauté for 4 minutes.
4. Beat eggs with cheese, milk, pepper and salt in a bowl.
5. Pour egg mixture over vegetables and bake in oven for 30 minutes.
6. Slices and serve.

NUTRITION:

- Calories 25
- Fat 16.7 g

- Carbohydrates 8 g
- Sugar 4 g
- Protein 22 g
- Cholesterol 257 mg

Pumpkin Muffins

Preparation Time: 10 minutes

Cooking Time: 25 minutes

Serve: 10

Ingredients:

- 4 eggs
- 1/2 cup pumpkin puree
- 1 tsp pumpkin pie spice
- 1/2 cup almond flour
- 1 tbsp baking powder
- 1 tsp vanilla
- 1/3 cup coconut oil, melted
- 2/3 cup swerve
- 1/2 cup coconut flour
- 1/2 tsp sea salt

Directions:

1. Preheat the oven to 350 F.
2. In a large bowl, stir together coconut flour, pumpkin pie spice, baking powder, swerve, almond flour, and sea salt.
3. Stir in eggs, vanilla, coconut oil, and pumpkin puree until well combined.
4. Pour batter into the greased muffin tray and bake in oven for 25 minutes.
5. Serve and enjoy.

NUTRITION:

- Calories 150
- Fat 13 g
- Carbohydrates 8g
- Sugar 2 g
- Protein 5 g
- Cholesterol 75 mg

Cheesy Spinach Quiche

Preparation Time: 10 minutes

Cooking Time: 7 Hours

Serve: 6

Ingredients:

- 8 eggs
- 2 cups fresh spinach
- 1/2 cup feta cheese, crumbled
- 1/2 cup parmesan cheese, shredded
- 1/4 cup cheddar cheese, shredded
- 3 garlic cloves, minced
- 2 cups unsweetened almond milk
- 1/4 tsp salt

Directions:

1. In a large bowl, whisk together eggs and almond milk.
2. Add spinach, parmesan cheese, feta cheese, garlic, and salt and stir well to combine.
3. Spray crock potwith cooking spray.
4. Pour egg mixture into the crock pot.
5. Sprinkle shredded cheddar cheese over the top of egg mixture.
6. Cover and cook on low for 7 hours.

NUTRITION:

- Calories 365
- Fat 32.5 g
- Carbohydrates 7 g
- Sugar 4 g
- Protein 16.1 g
- Cholesterol 249 mg

Chapter 12: Meat And Fish Dishes

Bacon Cheeseburger

Preparation Time: 5 minutes

Cooking Time: 15 minutes

Servings: 1

INGREDIENTS:

- 1/4 pound lean ground beef
- ¼ cup chopped yellow onion
- 1/4 clove garlic, minced
- 1/4 tablespoon yellow mustard
- 1/4 tablespoon Worcestershire sauce
- 1/8 teaspoon salt
- Cooking spray
- 1 ultra-thin slice cheddar cheese, cut into six equal-sized rectangular pieces
- 1piece of turkey bacon, each cut into eight evenly sized rectangular pieces
- 3 dill pickle chips
- 2 cherry tomatoes, sliced in half

DIRECTIONS:

1. Heat

2. Combine the garlic, salt, onion, Worcestershire sauce, and beef in a medium-sized bowl, and mix well.

3. Form mixture into 24 small meatballs. Put meatballs onto a foil-lined baking sheet and cook for 12–15 minutes. Leave oven.

4. Top every meatball with a piece of cheese, then go back to the oven till cheese melts, about 2 to 3 minutes. Let meatballs cool.

5. To assemble bites: on a toothpick layer, a cheese-covered meatball, piece of bacon, piece of lettuce, pickle chip, and a tomato half.

NUTRITION:

- **Calories:** 303
- **Protein:** 15g
- **Carbohydrates:** 30g
- **Fats:** 14g

Chicken Lo Mein

Preparation Time: 15 minutes

Cooking Time: 15 minutes

Servings: 1

INGREDIENTS:

- 1/2 tablespoon + 1/2 teaspoon sesame oil, divided
- 220g boneless. skinless chicken breasts, sliced
- ¼ teaspoon ground black pepper
- 1/4 tablespoon soy sauce
- 1/4 tablespoon oyster sauce

- 1/4 garlic clove, minced
- 1/2 teaspoon fresh ginger root
- 1/2 spring onions, trimmed and sliced with white and green parts separated
- 25g fresh mushrooms, divided
- 1/4 medium red bell pepper, membranes, and seeds removed
- 1/2 medium zucchinis (400g), cut, sliced

DIRECTIONS:

1. In a skillet, heat one-teaspoon sesame oil over medium-high heat. Put the shredded chicken, season with black pepper, and cook until chicken is done (internal temperature about 165°F). Dismiss from wok or skillet and set aside.

2. While the chicken cooks, prepare the sauce by combining the oyster sauce, soy sauce, and two tablespoons sesame oil in a bowl and whisking together. Set aside.

3. With the same skillet used to cook the chicken, heat one teaspoon sesame oil and put the garlic, ginger, and white spring onion pieces; cook until fragrant, about 1 minute. Put the mushrooms and bell peppers and continue to cook until just tender, about 3 minutes. Add zucchini noodles and toss to combine.

4. Pour in the sauce and put the chicken; cook until zucchini is tender, and the mixture should be heated by about 3 to 5 minutes.

5. Garnish with green parts of spring onions.

NUTRITION:

- **Calories:** 330
- **Protein:** 48g
- **Carbohydrates:** 9g
- **Fats:** 10g

Eggplant Parmesan with Chops

Preparation Time: 5 minutes

Cooking Time: 40 minutes

Servings: 1

INGREDIENTS:

- Bell peppers any color
- Mushrooms
- Vegetable broth
- Cooking spray
- Pepper
- Salt
- 1/2 packet optavia pancake mix
- 1/3 large eggplant
- Parmesan cheese
- Pork chops

DIRECTIONS:

1. Using a non-stick pan, fry the pork chops. You should be using the cooking spray, then spray for 7 minutes each side.

2. You also need to spray the glass cooking pan and lay chops on the bottom.

3. Followed by bell peppers around chops.

4. Put the mushrooms around chops.

5. Next, place vegetable broth over chops filling the pan 1/4 inch from the bottom.

6. Put it in the oven and bake at 350 degrees for 30 minutes.

7. Make sure to peel the eggplant and slice.

8. Mix pancake batter as directed and add 1/8 teaspoon baking powder and two egg whites.

9. Then, mix and dip eggplant in batter fry until golden brown, set aside.

10. Remove chops from oven let cool.

11. Arrange 1/2 cup eggplant and 5-oz. peppers on a plate, scoop 1/4 cup marinara on top of the pork chop.

12. Top with 1/4 cup parmesan cheese.

13. Enjoy! It makes three green servings and one lean serving. Mushroom is an extra 1/2 cup; otherwise, just use it for flavor—put in the microwave for 30 seconds, serve hot.

NUTRITION:

- **Calories:** 250
- **Carbohydrates:** 14.5g
- **Fats:** 15.9g
- **Protein:** 25g

Chicken Chili

Preparation Time: 10 minutes

Cooking Time: 30 minutes

Servings: 1

INGREDIENTS:

- 1(¼ pound) boneless chicken breast, cut into bite-size pieces
- 1/4 tablespoon olive oil
- 1/4 cup green spring onion, diced
- 1/3 cup bell pepper, seeded and chopped
- ½ cup jalapenos, seeded and diced
- ½ cloves garlic, minced
- ½ teaspoon salt

- 1/4 teaspoon ground cumin

- 1/4 teaspoon coriander

- 1 cup chicken broth

- 1/2 cup water

- ½(7-oz.) cans green chilies

- 1 tablespoon thick canned coconut milk, chopped green onions, and coriander for garnish

DIRECTIONS:

1. Mince the chicken and veggies. Then place a big pot over medium-high heat. Put the peppers, oil, onions, jalapeno, and garlic up.

2. Sauté for 5 minutes, then put the chicken, spices, and salt. Sauté additional 5–8 minutes until chicken is cooked well. Place the green chilies, broth, and coconut milk.

3. Bring to the boil. Cook for 15–20 minutes and shred chicken. Serve topped with green onions and coriander.

NUTRITION:

- **Calories:** 226

- **Protein:** 20g

- **Carbohydrates:** 19g

- **Fats:** 8g

Asparagus and Crabmeat Frittata

Preparation Time: 10–15 minutes

Cooking Time: 15–20 minutes

Servings: 1

INGREDIENTS:

- 1½ tablespoon extra-virgin olive oil

- 1 pound asparagus

- 1/2 cups liquid egg substitute

- 1/2 teaspoon salt

- 1 ½ teaspoon black pepper

- ¼ cup basil chopped

- 1/2 teaspoon sweet paprika

- 1/2 pound lump crabmeat

- 1/2 tablespoon finely cut chives

DIRECTIONS:

1. Deter the tough ends of the asparagus and cut it into bite-sized pieces.

2. Preheat an oven to 375°F.

3. In a 12-Inch to a 14-inch oven-proof, non-stick skillet, warm the olive oil and sweat the asparagus until tender—season with pepper, paprika, and salt.

4. In a mixing bowl, add the chives, crabmeat, and basil.

5. Pour in the liquid egg substitute and mix until combined.

6. With the cooked asparagus, pour the crab and egg mixture into the skillet then stir to combine. Bake over low to medium heat until the eggs start bubbling.

7. Place the skillet inside the oven. Then, bake for about 15–20 minutes. Wait until the eggs are golden brown. Serve the dish warm.

NUTRITION:

- **Calories:** 340

- **Protein:** 50g

- **Carbohydrates:** 14g

- Fats: **10g**

Mexican Cauliflower Rice

Preparation Time: 10 minutes

Cooking Time: 10 minutes

Serve: 3

Ingredients:

- 1 large cauliflower head, cut into florets
- 2 garlic cloves, minced
- 1 onion, diced
- 1 tbsp olive oil
- 1/4 cup vegetable broth
- 3 tbsp tomato paste
- 1/2 tsp cumin
- 1 tsp salt

Directions:

- Add cauliflower in food processor and process until it looks like rice.
- Heat oil in a pan over medium heat.
- Add onion and garlic and sauté for 3 minutes.
- Add cauliflower rice, cumin, and salt and stir well.
- Add broth and tomato paste and stir until well combined.
- Serve and enjoy.

Nutritional Value (Amount per Serving):

1. Calories 90
2. Fat 5 g
3. Carbohydrates 10 g
4. Sugar 4 g
5. Protein 3 g
6. Cholesterol 0 mg

Balsamic Zucchini Noodles

Preparation Time: 10 minutes

Cooking Time: 15 minutes

Serve: 4

Ingredients:

- 4 zucchinis, spiralized using a slicer
- 1 1/2 tbsp balsamic vinegar
- 1/4 cup fresh basil leaves, chopped
- 4 mozzarella balls, quartered
- 1 1/2 cups cherry tomatoes, halved
- 2 tbsp olive oil
- Pepper
- Salt

Directions:

1. Add zucchini noodles in a bowl and season with pepper and salt. Set aside for 10 minutes.
2. Add mozzarella, tomatoes, and basil and toss well.
3. Drizzle with oil and balsamic vinegar.
4. Serve and enjoy.

Nutritional Value (Amount per Serving):

- Calories 222
- Fat 15 g
- Carbohydrates 10 g
- Sugar 5.8 g
- Protein 9.5 g
- Cholesterol 13 mg

Cauliflower Broccoli Rice

Preparation Time: 10 minutes

Cooking Time: 8 minutes

Serve: 4

Ingredients:

- 1 cup broccoli, process into rice
- 3 cups cauliflower rice
- 1/4 cup mascarpone cheese
- 1/2 cup parmesan cheese, shredded
- 1/8 tsp ground cinnamon
- ¼ tsp garlic powder
- ¼ tsp onion powder
- 1/4 tsp pepper
- 1 tbsp butter, melted
- 1/2 tsp salt

Directions:

1. In a heat-safe bowl, mix together cauliflower, nutmeg, garlic powder, onion powder, butter, broccoli, pepper, and salt and microwave for 4 minutes.
2. Stir well and microwave for 2 minutes more.
3. Add cheese and microwave for 2 minutes.
4. Add mascarpone cheese and stir until it looks creamy.
5. Serve and enjoy.

Nutritional Value (Amount per Serving):

- Calories 135
- Fat 10 g
- Carbohydrates 6 g

- Sugar 2 g
- Protein 8 g
- Cholesterol 30 mg

Cheesy Cauliflower Broccoli Risotto

Preparation Time: 10 minutes

Cooking Time: 15 minutes

Serve: 2

Ingredients:

- 2 cups broccoli florets
- 1 cauliflower head, cut into florets
- 2 green onion, chopped
- 1/2 cup parmesan cheese, grated
- 2 tbsp heavy cream
- 1/2 tbsp lemon zest
- 1/2 cup vegetable stock
- 2 tbsp butter
- 1/2 tsp pepper
- 1/2 tsp salt

Directions:

1. Add cauliflower and broccoli florets into the food processor and process until it looks like rice.
2. Melt butter in a saucepan over medium heat. Add onion and sauté for 2 minutes.
3. Add broccoli and cauliflower rice and sauté for 2-3 minutes.
4. Add stock and cover and cook for 10 minutes.
5. Add cheese and heavy cream, and lemon zest and stir until cheese is melted.
6. Serve and enjoy.

Nutritional Value (Amount per Serving):

- Calories 315
- Fat 22 g
- Carbohydrates 12 g
- Sugar 5 g
- Protein 15 g
- Cholesterol 60 mg

Tasty Creamy Spinach

Preparation Time: 10 minutes

Cooking Time: 20 minutes

Serve: 6

Ingredients:

- 1 lb fresh spinach
- 1 tbsp onion, minced
- 8 oz cream cheese
- 6 oz cheddar cheese, shredded
- 1/2 tsp garlic powder
- Pepper
- Salt

Directions:

1. Preheat the oven to 400 F.
2. Spray pan with cooking spray and heat over medium heat.
3. Add spinach to the pan and cook until wilted.
4. Add cream cheese, garlic powder, and onion and stir until cheese is melted.
5. Remove pan from heat and add cheddar cheese and season with pepper and salt.
6. Pour spinach mixture into the greased baking dish and bake for 20 minutes.
7. Serve and enjoy.

Nutritional Value (Amount per Serving):

- Calories 250
- Fat 20 g
- Carbohydrates 5 g
- Sugar 1.5 g
- Protein 12 g
- Cholesterol 75 mg

Cauliflower Mash

Preparation Time: 10 minutes

Cooking Time: 10 minutes

Serve: 4

Ingredients:

- 1 lb cauliflower, cut into florets
- 1 tbsp lemon juice
- ¼ tsp onion powder
- 3 oz parmesan cheese, grated
- 4 oz butter
- ½ tsp garlic powder
- Pepper
- Salt

Directions:

1. Boil cauliflower florets until tender. Drain well.
2. Add cooked cauliflower into the blender with remaining ingredients and blend until smooth.
3. Serve and enjoy.

Nutritional Value (Amount per Serving):

- Calories 300
- Fat 28 g
- Carbohydrates 7 g
- Sugar 3 g
- Protein 10 g
- Cholesterol 75 mg

Roasted Broccoli

Preparation Time: 10 minutes

Cooking Time: 15 minutes

Scrve: 4

Ingredients:

- 2 lbs broccoli, cut into florets
- 3 tbsp olive oil
- 1 tbsp lemon juice
- 1/4 cup parmesan cheese, grated
- ¼ cup almonds, sliced and toasted
- 3 garlic cloves, sliced
- ½ tsp red pepper flakes
- 1/4 tsp pepper
- 1/4 tsp salt

Directions:

1. Preheat the oven to 425 F.
2. Add broccoli, pepper, salt, garlic, and oil in large bowl and toss well.
3. Spread broccoli on baking tray and roast in for 20 minutes.
4. Add lemon juice, grated cheese, red pepper flakes and almonds over broccoli and toss well.

5. Serve and enjoy.

Nutritional Value (Amount per Serving):

- Calories 205
- Fat 16 g
- Carbohydrates 13 g
- Sugar 3 g
- Protein 7.5 g
- Cholesterol 6 mg

Stir Fried Broccoli with Mushroom

Preparation Time: 10 minutes

Cooking Time: 20 minutes

Serve: 4

Ingredients:

- 2 cups broccoli, cut into florets
- 1 1/2 tsp fresh ginger, grated
- 1/4 tsp red pepper flakes
- 2 cups mushrooms, sliced
- 2 garlic cloves, minced
- 1 small onion, chopped
- 2 tbsp balsamic vinegar
- 1/2 tbsp sesame seeds
- 2 tbsp soy sauce, low-sodium
- 1/4 cup cashews
- 1 medium carrot, shredded
- 3 tbsp water

Directions:

1. Heat large pan over high heat.
2. Add broccoli, water, ginger, red pepper, mushrooms, garlic, and onion and cook until soft softened.
3. Add carrots, soy sauce, vinegar, and cashews. Stir well and simmer for 2 minutes.
4. Garnish with sesame seeds and serve

Nutritional Value (Amount per Serving):

- Calories 105
- Fat 5 g
- Carbohydrates 12 g
- Sugar 3 g
- Protein 5 g
- Cholesterol 0 mg

Flavors Zucchini Gratin

Preparation Time: 10 minutes

Cooking Time: 50 minutes

Serve: 9

Ingredients:

- 4 cups zucchini, sliced
- 2 tbsp butter
- 1 1/2 cups pepper jack cheese, shredded
- 1 onion, sliced
- ¼ tsp onion powder
- 1/2 cup heavy cream
- 1/2 tsp garlic powder
- Pepper
- Salt

Directions:

1. Preheat the oven to 375 F.
2. Add 1/3 sliced onion and zucchini in pan and season with pepper and salt.
3. Sprinkle 1/2 cup cheese on top of onion and zucchini.
4. In a baking dish, combine together heavy cream, butter, garlic powder, and onion powder and microwave for 1 minute.
5. Pour heavy cream mixture over sliced zucchini and onion.
6. Bake for 45 minutes.
7. Serve and enjoy.

Nutritional Value (Amount per Serving):

- Calories 85
- Fat 6 g
- Carbohydrates 3 g
- Sugar 1 g
- Protein 1 g
- Cholesterol 15 mg

Delicious Pumpkin Risotto

Preparation Time: 10 minutes

Cooking Time: 5 minutes

Serve: 1

Ingredients:

- 1/4 cup pumpkin, grated
- 1 tbsp butter
- 1/2 cup water
- 1 cup cauliflower, grated
- 2 garlic cloves, chopped

- 1/8 tsp cinnamon
- Pepper
- Salt

Directions:

1. Melt butter in a pan over medium heat.
2. Add garlic, cauliflower, cinnamon and pumpkin into the pan and season with pepper and salt.
3. Cook until lightly softened. Add water and cook until done.
4. Serve and enjoy.

Nutritional Value (Amount per Serving):

- Calories 155
- Fat 11 g
- Carbohydrates 11 g
- Sugar 4.5 g
- Protein 3.2 g
- Cholesterol 30 mg

Chapter 13: Smoothies And Breakfasts

Protein Oatcakes

Preparation Time: 10 minutes

Cooking Time: 5 minutes

Servings: 1

INGREDIENTS:

- 70g oatmeal
- 15g protein
- 1 egg white
- ½ cup water
- ½ teaspoon cinnamon
- 60g curd
- 1 teaspoon cacao powder
- 15g sugar

DIRECTIONS:

1. Mix the oatmeal, protein, egg white, and water in a bowl.

2. Preheat a saucepan to medium heat.

3. Place the mixture into the saucepan.

4. While waiting, prepare the topping by mixing the curd, cinnamon, and sugar in a second bowl.

5. Remove the oatcake from the saucepan when it becomes golden-brown.

6. Serve on a plate.

7. Add the topping and cocoa powder.

NUTRITION:

- **Calories:** 440
- **Protein:** 1.1g
- **Fiber:** 0.8g
- **Carbohydrates:** 6.1g

Asian Scrambled Egg

Preparation Time: 10 minutes

Cooking Time: 10 minutes

Servings: 1

INGREDIENTS:

- 1 large egg
- 1/2 teaspoons light soy sauce
- 1/8 teaspoon white pepper
- 1 tablespoon vegetable oil

DIRECTIONS:

1. Beat the eggs in a bowl.

2. To the beaten egg, add soy sauce, one-teaspoon vegetable oil, and pepper.

3. Preheat a saucepan on high heat.

4. Add the two tablespoons oil to the saucepan.

5. Then add the mixture of the beaten egg.

6. The edges will begin to cook.

7. Lessen the heat to medium and carefully scramble the eggs.

8. Turn off heat and transfer into a bowl.

9. Serve hot and enjoy

NUTRITION:

- **Calories**: 200
- **Fat**: 6.7g
- **Protein**: 6.1g
- **Carbohydrates**: 1g

Artichoke Frittatas

Preparation Time: 10 minutes

Cooking Time: 30 minutes

Servings: 1

INGREDIENTS:

- 2.5 oz. dry spinach
- 1/4 red bell pepper
- Artichoke (drain the liquid)
- Green onions
- Dried tomatoes
- Two eggs
- Italian seasoning
- Salt

- Pepper

DIRECTIONS:

1. Preheat oven to medium heat.

2. Brush a bit of oil on the cast-iron skillet.

3. Mix all the vegetables.

4. Add some seasoning.

5. Spread the vegetables evenly in the pan.

6. Whisk the eggs and add some milk.

7. Add some salt and pepper.

8. Mix in some cheese (helps to make it fluffier).

9. Pour the egg mixture in the saucepan.

10. Place the pan inside the oven for about 30 minutes.

11. Enjoy!

NUTRITION:

- **Calories:** 160
- **Protein:** 7g
- **Carbohydrates:** 4g
- **Fat:** 3.5g

Zucchini Frittata

Preparation Time: 20 minutes

Cooking Time: 20 minutes

Servings: 1

INGREDIENTS:

- 2 large zucchinis
- 1½ teaspoon of salt
- 2 eggs
- ½ cup chopped green onions
- 1 cup flour
- ½ teaspoon of black pepper
- 1 teaspoon of baking powder
- 2 tablespoons of oil

DIRECTIONS:

1. Wash the two zucchinis.
2. Cut off the zucchinis on its ends and grate them in a large mixing bowl.
3. Stir in 1 teaspoon of salt and set aside for about 10 minutes (The salt helps to draw out the water from the zucchinis).
4. Squeeze dry the grated zucchinis to remove as much water as possible.
5. Then followed by the two whole eggs and the chopped green onions.
6. In a bowl, mix a cup flour, ½ teaspoon of salt, ½ teaspoon of black pepper, and one teaspoon of baking powder.
7. Next, pour the contents of the smaller bowl to those of the larger bowl containing the grated zucchinis.
8. Stir them all together and make sure they are well mixed.
9. Preheat a saucepan to medium temperature and add two tablespoons of oil.

10. Add the zucchini mixture a heaping tablespoonful at a time.

11. Sauté the mixture for about 4 minutes on each side, to achieve a golden-brown color.

12. Add more oil to the pan if needed.

13. Serve and enjoy!

NUTRITION:

- **Calories:** 200
- **Protein:** 7g
- **Carbohydrates:** 4g
- **Fat:** 3.5g

Orange Ricotta Pancakes

Preparation Time: 10 minutes

Cooking Time: 5 minutes

Servings: 1

INGREDIENTS:

- ¾ cup all-purpose flour
- ½ tablespoon baking powder
- 2 teaspoons sugar
- ½ teaspoon salt
- 3 separated eggs
- 1 cup fresh ricotta
- ¾ cup whole milk
- ½ teaspoon pure vanilla extract
- 1 large ripe orange

DIRECTIONS:

1. Mix the flour, baking powder, sugar in a large bowl.
2. Add a pinch of salt.
3. In a separate bowl, whisk egg yolk, ricotta, milk, orange zest, and orange juice.
4. Add some vanilla extract for additional flavor.
5. Followed by the dry ingredients to the ricotta mixture and mix adequately.
6. Stir the egg white in a different bowl, and then gently fold it in the ricotta mixture.
7. Preheat saucepan to medium heat and brush with some butter until evenly spread.
8. Use a measuring cup to drop the batter onto the saucepan, ensure the pan is not crowded.
9. Allow cooking for 2 minutes.
10. Flip the food when you notice the edges begin to set, and bubbles form in the center.

11. Cook the meat for another 1 to 2 minutes.

12. Serve with any toppings of your choice.

NUTRITION:

- **Calories:** 160
- **Fat:** 10g
- **Carbohydrate:** 28g
- **Protein:** 6g

Chocolate Sweet Potato Pudding

Preparation Time: 5 minutes

Cooking Time: 2 minutes

Servings: 1

INGREDIENTS:

- 2 well-cooked sweet potatoes
- 2 tablespoons cocoa powder
- 2 tablespoons maple syrup
- ¼ cups plant-based milk (for example, almond milk)
- ¼ tablespoons salt
- ¼ tablespoons vanilla extract

DIRECTIONS:

1. Inside the food processor, put all the ingredients.

2. Blend thoroughly for about 30 seconds to 1 minute.

3. Voilà!

NUTRITION:

- **Calories:** 200

- **Fat:** 1.5g
- **Carbohydrates:** 23.4g
- **Fiber:** 1.3g

Peanut Butter and Protein Pancake

Preparation Time: 10 minutes

Cooking Time: 15 minutes

Servings: 1

INGREDIENTS:

- ½ cup oat flour
- ½ cup gluten-free chocolate pancake mix
- ½ cup almond milk
- 1 egg
- 1 tablespoon coconut water
- 1 tablespoon peanut butter
- Fresh fruits slices

DIRECTIONS:

1. Preheat a saucepan to medium heat.
2. Mix the flour and the pancake mix in a mixing bowl.
3. Mix the almond milk and eggs with coconut water in another bowl.
4. Mix the dry and wet ingredients thoroughly to form a delicate batter.
5. Spray the preheated saucepan with some coconut oil.
6. Put the batter into the saucepan with a measuring cup and allow it to cook for a few minutes.
7. Allow to cool and top with peanut butter and fresh fruit slices.

NUTRITION:

- **Calories:** 380
- **Protein:** 22g
- **Carbohydrates:** 16g

Tex-Mex Tofu Breakfast Tacos

Preparation Time: 10 minutes

Cooking Time: 15 minutes

Servings: 1

INGREDIENTS:

- 8 oz. firm tofu
- 1 cup well-cooked black bean
- 1/4 red onion
- 1 cup fresh coriander
- 1 ripe avocado
- 1/2 cup salsa
- 1 medium-sized lime
- 5 whole corn tortillas
- 1/2 teaspoon garlic powder
- 1/2 teaspoon chili powder
- 1/8 teaspoon of sea salt
- 1 tablespoon salsa
- 1 tablespoon water

DIRECTIONS:

1. Dice the red onions, avocados, coriander, and keep in separate bowls.
2. Also, slice the limes and keep in individual bowls.
3. In a clean towel. Wrap the tofu and place under a cast-iron skillet.

4. In the meantime, heat a saucepan to medium heat.

5. Cook the black beans in the saucepan, add a little amount of salt, cumin, and chili powder.

6. Then decrease the heat to a low simmer and set aside.

7. Add the tofu spices and salsa into a bowl, then add some water and set aside.

8. Heat another skillet to medium heat.

9. Pour some oil into the skillet, and then crumble the tofu into it.

10. Stir-fry for about 5 minutes until the tofu begins to brown.

11. Add some seasoning and continue to cook for about 5 to 10 minutes, and then set aside.

12. Heat the tortillas in oven to 250°F.

13. Top the tortillas with tofu scramble, avocado, salsa, coriander, black beans, and lime juice.

14. Serve immediately.

NUTRITION:

- **Calories:** 350
- **Fat:** 6.5g
- **Carbohydrates:** 23.6g
- **Protein:** 21.5g

Conclusion

You had reached the end of this book. You now know a lot about the Optavia Diet and even about recipes for this diet. I do hope you had already cooked several recipes. Will you agree with me that they are delicious?

Nevertheless, the diet is repetitive, costly, and doesn't cover all dietary needs. Another point is that extended calorie restriction may lead to nutrient deficiencies and other risky health concerns.

Although the program promotes fat loss and short-term weight loss, further research is required to evaluate the level of lifestyle changes it needs for long-term success.

If you ever succeed on the structure and need to get fit rapidly, the Optavia Diet could be a solid match for you.

Before you start any feast substitution diet, cautiously consider whether you can sensibly tail it, choose how much cash you can contribute, and decide the level of craving and interference in your social routine that you feel good about.

If you ever will settle on Optavia and prevail with your transient weight loss objectives, ensure you become taught about smart dieting to keep the weight in the long-term because that is the common mishap of people who follow this diet. Always maintain.

It had been a long journey for finding the most appropriate diet or learning recipes that you may use. You may continue with your quest on the Optavia Diet.

All the best!

CPSIA information can be obtained
at www.ICGtesting.com
Printed in the USA
LVHW020506121220
674004LV00009B/198